THE
FORGOTTEN
COMMANDMENT

JOE W. GRESHAM

THE FOURTH
ANGEL'S PUBLISHING

2705 BIWAY · FORT WORTH, TEXAS 76114

Edited by
Lisa Loggins

Cover design by
Hartland Publications

Printed by
Hartland Publications
Rapidan, Virginia

ISBN 978-0-9712097-8-7

TABLE OF CONTENTS

CHAPTER 1

THE LORD'S DAY

Revelation 1:10 is a verse that many have taken out of context in an attempt to support an erroneous, non-biblical, man-made tradition. The prophet says simply that he "was in the Spirit on the Lord's day." He does not say which day of the week this is, but simply tells us there is one period of twenty-four hours in each week that is different from the other six days, and this period of time is considered by the Lord to be His day.

For one to ascertain which day of the week the Lord accounts as His day, there is no one better to ask than the Lord Himself, and he clearly tells us that He is Lord of the "Sabbath day" (Matthew 12:8; Mark 2:28). We also find at the creation of this world "God blessed the seventh day, and sanctified it" (Genesis 2:1-3) as a memorial of His creation.

This special day was so important to God that He included it in the Ten Commandments some 2,500 years later in the clearest language possible. "Remember the Sabbath day, to keep it holy. Six days shalt thou labour, and do all thy work: But the seventh day is the Sabbath of the Lord thy God: in it thou shalt not do any work, thou, nor thy son, nor thy daughter, thy manservant, nor thy maidservant, nor thy cattle, nor thy stranger that is within thy gates: For in six days the Lord made heaven and earth, the sea, and all that in them is, and rested the seventh day: wherefore the Lord blessed the Sabbath day, and hallowed it" (Exodus 20:8-11). Some 800 years after Sinai the Lord called upon His people to stop desecrating "the Sabbath" by doing their "pleasure on My holy day" (Isaiah 58:13).

In light of all this Bible evidence, and without any Scripture to support their erroneous position, there are many who still insist that the "Lord's day" refers to Sunday, or that the first day of the week is really the seventh day of the Bible. However, the word of God makes very clear which day of the week is the first and which is the seventh.

There is great unanimity among Christians today that the day of Jesus' crucifixion was Friday. The Christian celebration of that event is even called "Good Friday." The same unanimity exists as to the day of His resurrection, which Christianity refers to as "Easter Sunday." Now, in the Scripture, we find that the day on which Jesus was crucified is called "the preparation" day and preceded the Sabbath day (Luke 23:54). As Jesus was taken from the cross and carried to the tomb on "Good Friday" the women followed, and then returned to prepare spices and ointments for the burial, but instead of returning to the tomb they "rested the Sabbath day according to the commandment" (Luke 23:55-56). After the Sabbath was over they returned to the tomb "upon the first day of the week, very early in the morning" (Luke 24:1).

The word of God is so simple that even a young child can easily discern that the "Lord's day" is the seventh-day Sabbath of the fourth commandment, or the day that comes between "Good Friday" and "Easter Sunday."

Even though the Scriptures are clear that the Sabbath was made for all mankind (Mark 2:27), some have tried to say the Sabbath was only a Jewish institution. This is further shown to be totally without merit inasmuch as it was given at creation (Genesis 2:1-3), thousands of years before Moses or any Jew.

CHAPTER 2

RIDICULOUS REASONS FOR REJECTION

Others claim that one should keep Sunday holy in honor of the resurrection of Christ. This immediately presents two insurmountable problems:

1. How can anyone keep holy that which God has not made holy?
2. Jesus said that baptism is the ordinance one is to practice to honor His resurrection. Romans 6:3-4

Some have even said, "I keep every day alike." This, too, presents problems of tremendous magnitude. To observe them all alike is deliberate ignorance and disobedience, for He did not make them all alike. He made one different from the other six and said to remember to keep it holy. Six days are man's in which to labor and get his work done. The Sabbath is God's holy day and we are to cease from our labors (Hebrews 4:9-11). It is an absolute impossibility to keep alike that which is not alike. Furthermore, it is a lie to claim that one can do it and rebellion to attempt to do so.

There are several significant Bible facts that so many Christians either overlook or ignore today:

1. While Jesus was on this earth He kept the Sabbath. Luke 4:16.
2. In speaking of an event 40 years after His death, He showed He still intended for His people to be keeping the Sabbath. Matthew 24:20
3. The Gentile Christians kept the Sabbath. Acts 13:42.
4. Nearly the whole city came the next Sabbath. Acts 13:44.
5. The people came together every Sabbath. Acts 18:4.
6. Paul's custom, or manner, was like that of Jesus' in observing the Sabbath. Acts 17:2.
7. God's law, including His Sabbath, will endure forever; even in the earth made new. Isaiah 66:22-23.
8. It has always been a sign between God and His people.

Ezekiel 20:12, 19, 20.

9. Jesus says that when one knowingly replaces His commandments with man-made traditions, that person's religion becomes worthless. Matthew 15:3, 9.

History reveals that man ordered a change of God's day of worship from Saturday to Sunday at the Council of Laodicea in A.D. 336, and today many worship on Sunday, thereby following man-made tradition instead of the commandments of God. Remember, it is not for man to say "I know what you say, Lord, but I have decided that something else will work just as well." It is most clear that at all times "we ought to obey God rather than men" (Acts 5:29).

Jesus says, "If you love me, keep my commandments" (John 14:15 NKJV). His call to His people is still the same today as it was centuries ago. "Choose you this day whom ye will serve" (Joshua 24:15). If you truly love Him, let your answer be: "The Lord our God will we serve, and His voice will we obey" (Joshua 24:24).

Some have attempted to find support for observance of the man-made Sunday/Sabbath by taking a few Bible verses out of context. Therefore it is expedient that we consider these verses.

CHAPTER 3

SUNDAY IN THE NEW TESTAMENT

There are only eight texts in the entire New Testament that refer to the first day of the week. The first reference to the first day is found in Matthew 28:1 and is simply Matthew's account of the resurrection.

"In the end of the sabbath, as it began to dawn toward the first day of the week, came Mary Magdalene and the other Mary to see the sepulchre."

Two other references are found in the Gospel of Mark. Mark 16:1-2 contains the second mention of the first day and is Mark's record of the resurrection, and as with Matthew, contains not even the slightest hint of a change of the day of worship. "And when the sabbath was past, Mary Magdalene, and Mary the mother of James, and Salome, had bought sweet spices, that they might come and anoint him. And very early in the morning the first day of the week, they came unto the sepulchre at the rising of the sun."

The third reference, found in Mark 16:9, simply informs us that after His resurrection the first person He appeared to was Mary. "Now when Jesus was risen early the first day of the week, he appeared first to Mary Magdalene, out of whom he had cast seven devils." Verses 10-13 tells us, that far from celebrating the resurrection, they did not even believe that Jesus was risen from the dead when others reported He had appeared to them. "And she went and told them that had been with him, as they mourned and wept. And they, when they had heard that he was alive, and had been seen of her, believed not. After that he appeared in another form unto two of them, as they walked, and went into the country. And they went and told it unto the residue: neither believed they them." As a result of their unbelief Jesus rebuked them when He later appeared to the group. "Afterward he appeared unto the eleven as they sat at meat, and upbraided them with their unbelief and hardness of heart, because they believed not them which had seen him after he was risen" (Mark 16:14).

The fourth mention of the first day is found in Luke's record of the resurrection. "Now upon the first day of the week, very early in the morning, they came unto the sepulchre, bringing the spices which they had prepared, and certain others with them" (Luke 24:1). Again we find the others were not honoring the resurrection, but rather disbelieved the women and considered their story an idle tale. "And they remembered his words, And returned from the sepulchre, and told all these things unto the eleven, and to all the rest. It was Mary Magdalene, and Joanna, and Mary the mother of James, and other women that were with them, which told these things unto the apostles. And their words seemed to them as idle tales, and they believed them not" (Luke 24:8-11). If anything, this passage shows the first day was considered a regular day in which the women had come to the tomb to do that which they would not do on the holy Sabbath. "This man (Joseph of Arimathaea) went unto Pilate, and begged the body of Jesus. And he took it down, and wrapped it in linen, and laid it in a sepulchre that was hewn in stone, wherein never man before was laid. And that day was the preparation, and the sabbath drew on. And the women also, which came with him from Galilee, followed after, and beheld the sepulchre, and how his body was laid. And they returned, and prepared spices and ointments; and rested the sabbath day according to the commandment" (Luke 23:52-56).

John's reference to the resurrection contains the fifth reference, but again there is not not the slightest indication of a change in the day of worship. "The first day of the week cometh Mary Magdalene early, when it was yet dark, unto the sepulchre, and seeth the stone taken away from the sepulchre" (John 20:1).

Reference six to the first day is found in John 20:19. "Then the same day at evening, being the first day of the week, when the doors were shut where the disciples were assembled for fear of the Jews, came Jesus and stood in the midst, and saith unto them, Peace be unto you." Notice that the reason they were assembled was not for worship, or to even acknowledge the resurrection, but because they were afraid of the Jews. They were hiding.

Many have attempted to use Acts 20:7-10 to justify rejecting the fourth commandment and keep a man-made tradition. "And upon the first day of the week, when the disciples came together to break bread, Paul preached unto them, ready to depart on the morrow; and continued his speech until midnight. And there were many lights in the upper chamber, where they were gathered together. And there sat in a window a certain young man named Eutychus, being fallen into a deep sleep: and as Paul was long preaching, he sunk down with sleep, and fell down from the third loft, and was taken up dead. And Paul went down, and fell on him, and embracing him said, Trouble not yourselves; for his life is in him." Notice carefully several points in this seventh reference to the first day:

1. There were "many lights" because it was dark. It was an evening meeting.
2. Paul preached until midnight when a young man fell from a window.
3. Paul raised him to life and continued to preach until dawn.
4. At sunrise Paul walked 20 miles to Assos to meet others and sail to Mytilene.

This is a Saturday night meeting that continued until dawn on Sunday, as some modern translations show. Remember, the Bible reckons a day as beginning at sunset, or at evening (Genesis 1:5, 8, 13, 19, 23, 31). The Sabbath is to be observed from evening until evening (Leviticus 23:32). We still follow this practice for certain holidays such as Christmas Eve or New Year's Eve. It was not until the Synod of Diamper in 1599 the time-table was changed to begin the day at midnight. Man can change the clocks, but he can't change the sun.

Even without these irrefutable facts, simply because one

preaches on a certain day does not make that day holy. Only God can make something holy, and man can only keep holy that which God has made holy. The same is true with "breaking bread" for the early church did this daily (Acts 2:46).

The eighth and final reference that some use to try and defend disobeying the Sabbath commandment is found in 1 Corinthians 16:1-2. "Now concerning the collection for the saints, as I have given order to the churches of Galatia, even so do ye. Upon the first day of the week let every one of you lay by him in store, as God hath prospered him, that there be no gatherings when I come."

Many claim this proves that Sunday is holy because they took up a collection on that day. As a minister of the gospel of the Lord Jesus Christ I have, at one time or another, taken an offering on every day of the week. Does that make every day holy? Does taking an offering make a day holy? We have already seen that we can do nothing to make something holy. All we can do is keep holy that which God has made holy. This passage is instructing the believer to "lay by him in store" or lay aside money at home for the poor. Paul was not even there with them, but was coming to pick it up and take it to the believers in Jerusalem (Acts 11:29, 30).

There are many pastors and authors telling people they do not have to keep God's holy Sabbath. Each give different reasons; they are not even agreed among themselves. How much better it would be if they would just recognize the facts as they are, as history shows them to be. Remember, Sunday-keeping does not come from the Bible at all. It comes from the traditions of men and branded with paganism and rebellion against God.

Could it be that Jesus' question: "Why do ye also transgress the commandment of God by your tradition" (Matthew 15:3) applies to you? He says very clearly "ye have made the commandment of God of none effect by your tradition" (Matthew 15:6) and those who do worship Him in vain, "teaching for doctrines the commandments of men" (Matthew 15:9).

When Jesus comes there will be many professed Christians who will be surprised to hear Him say, "depart from Me, ye that work iniquity" (Matthew 7:21-23). Iniquity is sin. Sin is the transgression of the law (1 John 3:4). God's law contains the Sabbath commandment (Exodus 20:8-11). An appropriate paraphrase would be "Depart from Me, ye that reject My Sabbath and transgress My law."

The word of God warned that there would be "false teachers" who would "bring in damnable heresies" and "many shall follow their pernicious ways" and the "truth shall be evil spoken of" (2 Peter 2:1-2). Today people are told they do not need to keep the law: "The law has been abolished." "It has been nailed to the cross." "It was only for the Jews." "We don't need it because we are under grace." "The Sabbath is not important." "We should keep Sunday in honor of the resurrection." These are but a few of the diabolic declarations one hears today. "Look at how many keep Sunday and how few keep Saturday. The multitude can't be wrong." is their preposterous proclamation. The obedient have always been in the minority. Consider the flood. Where were the majority, in the ark or outside? At the crucifixion was it the majority or minority that cried out "Crucify Him"?

Hear the word of Jesus: "Strait is the gate, and narrow is the way, which leadeth unto life, and few there be that find it" (Matthew 7:14). "Fear not, LITTLE flock; for it is your Father's good pleasure to give you the kingdom" (Luke 12:32). His flock may be small, but it is comprised of those who hear His voice and follow Him (John 10:27). Hear His voice as it spoke from Sinai: "Remember the Sabbath day, to keep it holy" (Exodus 20:8). Hear Him as he pleads: "If ye love Me, keep My commandments" (John 14:15). Do you love Him? Are you willing to keep His commandments? Yes, the multitudes reject God's holy Sabbath as well as much of the rest of His word; but remember, the multitude was found outside the ark and it was the multitude that cried out "Crucify Him." Will you stand with the multitude or with Jesus?

CHAPTER 4

WHAT OTHERS SAY ABOUT THE SABBATH?

BAPTIST

"There was and is a commandment to keep holy the Sabbath day, but that Sabbath day was not Sunday. It will be said, however, and with some show of triumph, that the Sabbath was transferred from the seventh to the first day of the week, with all its duties, privileges, and sanctions. Earnestly desiring information on this subject, which I have studied for many years, I ask, Where can the record of such a transaction be found? Not in the New Testament, absolutely not. There is no Scriptural evidence of the change of the Sabbath institution from the seventh to the first day of the week...

"Of course, I quite well know that Sunday did come into use in early Christian history as a religious day, as we learn from the Christian Fathers and other sources. But what a pity that it comes branded with the mark of paganism, and christened with the name of the sun god, when adopted and sanctioned by the papal apostasy, and bequeathed as a sacred legacy to Protestantism!" Edward T. Hiscox, author of The Baptist Manual, in a paper read before a New York Ministers' Conference held Nov. 13, 1893

CHRISTIAN

"I do not believe that the Lord's day came in the room of the Jewish Sabbath, or that the Sabbath was changed from the seventh to the first day, for this plain reason, that where there is no testimony, there can be no faith. Now there is no testimony in all the oracles of heaven that the Sabbath was changed, or that the Lord's day came in the room of it .... There is no divine testimony that the Sabbath was changed, or that the Lord's day came in the room of it; therefore there can be no divine faith that the Sabbath was changed or that the Lord's day came in the room of it." Alexander Campbell (Candidus), in Washington

(Pa.) Reporter, Oct. 8, 1821

CHURCH OF ENGLAND
"There is no word, no hint, in the New Testament about abstaining from work on Sunday.... into the rest of Sunday no divine law enters....The observance of Ash Wednesday or Lent stands on exactly the same footing as the observance of Sunday." Canon Eyton. The Ten Commandments, pp. 52, 63, 65

CONGREGATIONALIST
"It is quite clear that, however rigidly or devoutly we may spend Sunday, we are not keeping the Sabbath... The Sabbath was founded on a specific, divine command. We can plead no such command for the observance of Sunday..... There is not a single sentence in the New Testament to suggest that we incur any penalty by violating the supposed sanctity of Sunday." R. W. Dale, The Ten Commandments, pp. 106, 107

LUTHERAN
"They [the Catholics] allege the Sabbath changed into Sunday, the Lord's day, contrary to the decalogue, as it appears; neither is there any example more boasted of than the changing of the Sabbath day. Great, say they, is the power and authority of the church, since it dispensed with one of the ten commandments." Augsburg Confession, art. XXVIII

METHODIST
"It is true there is no positive command for infant baptism... Nor is there any for keeping holy the first day of the week..." Rev. Amos Binney, Theological Compend., pp. 180, 181

PRESBYTERIAN
"The moral law doth for ever bind all, as well justified persons as others, to the obedience thereof, and that not only in regard of the matter contained in it, but also in respect of the

authority of God the Creator who gave it. Neither doth Christ in the gospel any way dissolve, but much strengthen, this obligation." The Constitution of the Presbyterian Church in the U.S.A.

ROMAN CATHOLIC

"Of course the Catholic church claims that the change was her act. It could not have been otherwise as none in those days would have dreamed of doing anything in matters spiritual and ecclesiastical and religious without her and the act is a mark of her ecclesiastical power and authority in religious matters." James Cardinal Gibbons, Letter, November 11, 1895

"Question: Which is the Sabbath day?

"Answer: Saturday is the Sabbath day.

"Question: Why do we observe Sunday instead of Saturday?

"Answer: We observe Sunday instead of Saturday because the Catholic Church, in the Council of Laodicea (A.D. 336), transferred the solemnity from Saturday to Sunday.

"Question: Have you any other way of proving that the church has power to institute festivals of precept?

"Answer: Had she not such power, she could not have substituted the observance of Sunday the first day of the week, for the observance of Saturday, the seventh day, a change for which there is no scriptural authority." Keenan, A Doctrinal Catechism, p. 174

"The Catholic Church for over one thousand years before the existence of a Protestant, by virtue of her divine mission, changed the day from Saturday to Sunday." The Catholic Mirror, September 23, 1893

"Nowhere in the Bible do we find that Christ or the Apostles ordered that the Sabbath be changed from Saturday to Sunday. We have the commandment of God given to Moses to keep holy the Sabbath day, that is the seventh day of the week, Saturday. Today most Christians keep Sunday because it has been revealed to us by the church (Catholic) outside the Bible." The Catholic

Virginian, October 3, 1947

"If you go to the Bible you find that the seventh day Sabbath was the original Sabbath, but there is one thing you must understand and that is that we Catholics take the stand that the Bible does not contain all truths necessary to salvation, but that tradition of the Fathers and acts taken by the church are of equal importance with the Bible. The early church Christians observed the seventh day of the week, Saturday, as the Sabbath. In the early day the early Christian fathers began advocating Sunday as the Sabbath in honour of the resurrection of Christ. Early church councils took certain actions changing to Sunday the Sabbath. There is no text in the Bible that gives authority for this change. Protestants broke away from the Catholic Church in the 15th and 16th centuries, but they did not go back to the Bible Sabbath: they are still following the Catholic Church in the observance of Sunday." Roger Holly, Bible Lectures: The Mark of the Beast, p. 12

"Question: What Bible authority is there for changing the Sabbath from the seventh to the first day of the week? Who gave the Pope the authority to change a command of God?

Answer: If the Bible is the only guide for the Christian, then the Seventh-Day Adventist is right in observing the Saturday with the Jews. But Catholics learn what to believe and do from the divine, infallible authority established by Jesus Christ, the Catholic Church. Is it not strange that those who make the Bible their only teacher should inconsistently follow in this matter the tradition of the Catholic Church?" Conway, The Question Box, pp. 254, 255

"You may read the Bible from Genesis to Revelation, and you will not find a single line authorizing the sanctification of Sunday. The Scriptures enforce the religious observance of Saturday, a day which we never sanctify." James Cardinal Gibbons, Faith of Our Fathers, p.89

"Sunday is founded not on Scripture, but on tradition, and is distinctly a Catholic institution. As there is no Scripture for the transfer of the day of rest from the last to the first day of the week, Protestants ought to keep their Sabbath on Saturday and thus leave Catholics in full possession of Sunday." The Catholic Record, September 17, 1891

"Reason and common sense demand the acceptance of one or another of these alternatives: either Protestantism and the keeping of Saturday, or Catholicity and the keeping of Sunday. Compromise is impossible." The Catholic Mirror, December 23, 1893

"Dear Sir: Regarding the change from the observance of the Jewish Sabbath to the Christian Sunday, I wish to draw your attention to the facts: "That Protestants, who accept the Bible as the only rule of faith and religion, should by all means go back to the observance of the Sabbath...We also say, that of all Protestants, the Seventh-day Adventists are the only group that reason correctly and are consistent with the teachings." Extension Magazine, April 1, 1929

HISTORY REVEALS

"The people of Constantinople, and almost everywhere, assemble together on the Sabbath, as well as on the first day of the week, which custom is never observed at Rome or Alexandria." Sozoman, a church historian of the fifth century, quoted in Bible Readings for the Home, p. 438

"Down even to the fifth century the observance of the Jewish Sabbath was continued in the Christian church, but with a rigor and solemnity gradually diminishing until it was wholly discontinued." Lyman Coleman, Ancient Christianity Exemplified, chapter 26, section 2

CHAPTER 5

ONE HUNDRED BIBLE FACTS

SIXTY BIBLE FACTS CONCERNING THE SEVENTH DAY

Why keep the Sabbath day? What is the object of the Sabbath? Who made it? When was it made, and for whom? Which day is the true Sabbath? Many keep the first day of the week, or Sunday. What Bible authority have they for this? Some keep the seventh day, or Saturday. What Scripture have they for that? Here are the facts about both days, as plainly stated in the Word of God:

1. After working the first six days of the week in creating this earth, the great God rested on the seventh day. (Genesis 2:1-3.)
2. This stamped that day as God's rest day, or Sabbath day, as Sabbath means rest. To illustrate: When a person is born on a certain day, that day becomes his birthday. So when God rested upon the seventh day, that day became His rest, or Sabbath, day.
3. Therefore the seventh day must always be God's Sabbath day. Can you change your birthday from the day on which you were born to one on which you were not born? No. Neither can you change God's rest day to a day on which He did not rest. Hence the seventh day is still God's Sabbath day.
4. The Creator blessed the seventh day. (Genesis 2:3.)
5. He sanctified the seventh day. (Exodus 20:11.)
6. He made it the Sabbath day in the Garden of Eden. (Genesis 2:1-3.)
7. It was made before the fall; hence it is not a type; for types were not introduced till after the fall.
8. Jesus says it was made for man (Mark 2:27), that is, for the human race, as the word man is here unlimited; hence, for the Gentile as well as for the Jew.

9. It is a memorial of creation. (Exodus 20:11; 31:17.) Every time we rest upon the seventh day, as God did at creation, we commemorate that grand event.

10. It was given to Adam, the head of the human race. (Mark 2:27; Genesis 2:1-3.)

11. Hence through him, as our representative, to all nations. (Acts 17:26.)

12. It is not a Jewish institution, for it was made 2,300 years before ever there was a Jew.

13. The Bible never calls it the Jewish Sabbath, but always "the Sabbath of the Lord thy God." Men should be cautious how they stigmatize God's holy rest day.

14. Evident reference is made to the Sabbath and the seven-day week all through the patriarchal age. (Genesis 2:1-3; 8:10, 12; 29:27, 28, etc.)

15. It was a part of God's law before Sinai. (Exodus 16:4, 27-29.)

16. God placed it in the heart of His moral law. (Exodus 20:1-17.) Why did He place it there if it was not like the other nine precepts, which everyone admits to be immutable?

17. The seventh-day Sabbath was commanded by the voice of the living God. (Deuteronomy 4:12, 13.)

18. He wrote the commandment with His own finger. (Exodus 31:18.)

19. He engraved it in the enduring stone, indicating its imperishable nature. (Deuteronomy 5:22.)

20. It was sacredly preserved in the ark in the holy of holies. (Deuteronomy 10:1-5.)

21. God forbade work upon the Sabbath, even in the most hurrying times. (Exodus 34:21.)

22. God destroyed the Israelites in the wilderness because they profaned the Sabbath. (Ezekiel 20:12, 13.)

23. It is the sign of the true God, by which we are to know Him from false gods. (Ezekiel 20:20.)

24. God promised that Jerusalem should stand forever if the Jews would keep the Sabbath. (Jeremiah 17:24, 25.)

25. He sent them into the Babylonish captivity for breaking it.

(Nehemiah 13:18)

26. He destroyed Jerusalem for its violation. (Jeremiah 17:27.)
27. God has pronounced a special blessing on all the Gentiles who will keep it. (Isaiah 56:6, 7.)
28. This is in the prophecy which refers wholly to the Christian dispensation. (See Isaiah 56.)
29. God has promised to bless all who keep the Sabbath. (Isaiah 56:2.)
30. The Lord requires us to call it "honourable." (Isaiah 58:13.) Beware, ye who take delight in calling it the "old Jewish Sabbath," "a yoke of bondage," etc.
31. After the holy Sabbath has been trodden down "many generations," it is to be restored in the last days. (Isaiah 58:12, 13.)
32. All the holy prophets kept the seventh day.
33. When the Son of God came, He kept the seventh day all His life. (Luke 4:16; John 15:10.) Thus He followed His Father's example at creation. Shall we not be safe in following the example of both the Father and the Son?
34. The seventh day is the Lord's day. (See Revelation 1:10; Mark 2:28; Isaiah 58:13; Exodus 20:10.)
35. Jesus was Lord of the Sabbath (Mark 2:28). This means He loves and protects it, just as the husband, who is lord of the wife, will love and cherish her (1 Peter 3:6).
36. He vindicated the Sabbath as a merciful institution designed for man's good. (Mark 2:23-28.)
37. Instead of abolishing the Sabbath, He carefully taught how it should be observed. (Matthew 12:1-13.)
38. He taught His disciples that they should do nothing upon the Sabbath day but what was "lawful." (Matthew 12:12.)
39. He instructed His apostles that the Sabbath should be prayerfully regarded forty years after His resurrection. (Matthew 24:20.)
40. The pious women who had been with Jesus carefully kept the seventh day after His death. (Luke 23:56.)
41. Thirty years after Christ's resurrection, the Holy Spirit

expressly calls it "the sabbath day." (Acts 13:14.)

42. Paul, the apostle to the Gentiles, called it the "sabbath day" in A.D. 45. (Acts 13:27.) Did not Paul know? Or shall we believe modern teachers, who affirm that it ceased to be the Sabbath at the resurrection of Christ?

43. Luke, the inspired Christian historian, writing as late as A.D. 62, calls it the "sabbath day." (Acts 13:44.)

44. The Gentile converts called it the Sabbath. (Acts 13:42.)

45. In the great Christian council, A.D. 49, in the presence of the apostles and thousands of disciples, James calls it the "sabbath day." (Acts 15:21.)

46. It was customary to hold prayer meetings upon that day. (Acts 16:13.)

47. Paul read the Scriptures in public meetings on that day. (Acts 17:2, 3.)

48. It was his custom to preach upon that day. (Acts 17:2, 3.)

49. The Book of Acts alone gives a record of his holding eighty-four meetings upon that day. (See Acts 13:14, 44; 16:13; 17:2; 18:4, 11.)

50. There was never any dispute between the Christians and the Jews about the Sabbath day. This is proof that the Christians still observed the same day that the Jews did.

51. In all their accusations against Paul, they never charged him with disregarding the Sabbath day. Why did they not, if he did not keep it?

52. But Paul himself expressly declared that he had kept the law. "Neither against the law of the Jews, neither against the temple, nor yet against Caesar, have I offended any thing at all." Acts 25:8. How could this be true if he had not kept the Sabbath?

53. The Sabbath is mentioned in the New Testament fifty-nine times, and always with respect, bearing the same title it had in the Old Testament, "the sabbath day."

54. Not a word is said anywhere in the New Testament about the Sabbath's being abolished, done away, changed, or anything of the kind.

55. God has never given permission to any man to work upon it. Reader, by what authority do you use the seventh day for common labor?
56. No Christian of the New Testament, either before or after the resurrection, ever did ordinary work upon the seventh day. Find one case of that kind, and we will yield the question. Why should we do differently from Bible Christians?
57. There is no record that God has ever removed His blessing or sanctification from the seventh day.
58. As the Sabbath was kept in Eden before the fall, so it will be observed eternally in the new earth after the restitution. (Isaiah 66:22, 23.)
59. The seventh-day Sabbath was an important part of the law of God, as it came from His own mouth, and was written by His own finger upon stone at Sinai. (See Exodus 20.) When Jesus began His work, He expressly declared that He had not come to destroy the law. "Think not that I am come to destroy the law, or the prophets." Matthew 5:17.
60. Jesus severely condemned the Pharisees as hypocrites for pretending to love God, while at the same time they made void one of the Ten Commandments by their tradition. The keeping of Sunday is only a tradition of men.

FORTY BIBLE FACTS CONCERNING THE FIRST DAY

1. The very first thing recorded in the Bible is work done on Sunday, the first day of the week. (Genesis 1:1-5.) This was done by the Creator Himself. If God made the earth on Sunday, can it be wicked for us to work on Sunday?
2. God commands men to work upon the first day of the week. (Exodus 20:8-11.) Is it wrong to obey God?
3. None of the patriarchs ever kept it.
4. None of the holy prophets ever kept it.
5. By the express command of God, His holy people used the first day of the week as a common working day for at least 4,000 years.

6. God Himself calls it a "working" day. (Ezekiel 46:1.)
7. God did not rest upon it.
8. He never blessed it.
9. Christ did not rest upon it.
10. Jesus was a carpenter (Mark 6:3), and worked at His trade until He was thirty years old. He kept the Sabbath and worked six days in the week, as all admit. Hence He did many a hard day's work on Sunday.
11. The apostles worked upon it during the same time.
12. The apostles never rested upon it.
13. Christ never blessed it.
14. It has never been blessed by any divine authority.
15. It has never been sanctified.
16. No law was ever given to enforce the keeping of it, hence it is no transgression to work upon it. "Where no law is, there is no transgression." Romans 4:15. (See also 1 John 3:4.)
17. The New Testament nowhere forbids work to be done on it.
18. No penalty is provided for its violation.
19. No blessing is promised for its observance.
20. No regulation is given as to how it ought to be observed. Would this be so if the Lord wished us to keep it?
21. It is never called the Christian Sabbath.
22. It is never called the Sabbath day at all.
23. It is never called the Lord's day.
24. It is never called even a rest day.
25. No sacred title whatever is applied to it. Then why should we call it holy?
26. It is simply called "first day of the week."
27. Jesus never mentioned it in any way, never took its name upon His lips, so far as the record shows.
28. The word Sunday never occurs in the Bible at all.
29. Neither God, Christ, nor inspired men ever said one word in favor of Sunday as a holy day.
30. The first day of the week is mentioned only eight times in all the New Testament. (Matthew 28:1; Mark 16:2, 9; Luke 24:1; John 20:1, 19; Acts 20:7; 1 Corinthians 16:2)

31. Six of these texts refer to the same first day of the week.
32. Paul directed the saints to look over their secular affairs on that day. (1 Corinthians 16:2.)
33. In all the New Testament we have a record of only one religious meeting held upon that day, and even this was a night meeting. (Acts 20:5-12.)
34. There is not an intimation that they ever held a meeting upon it before or after that.
35. It was not their custom to meet on that day.
36. There was no requirement to break bread on that day.
37. We have an account of only one instance in which it was done. (Acts 20:7.)
38. That was done in the night after midnight. (Verses 7-11.) Jesus celebrated it on Thursday evening (Luke 22), and the disciples sometimes did it every day (Acts 2:42-46).
39. The Bible nowhere says that the first day of the week commemorates the resurrection of Christ. This is a tradition of men, which contradicts the law of God. (Matthew 15:1-9.) Baptism commemorates the death, burial, and resurrection of Jesus. (Romans 6:3-5.)
40. Finally, the New Testament is totally silent with regard to any change of the Sabbath day or any sacredness for the first day.

Here are one hundred plain Bible facts upon this question, showing conclusively that the seventh day is the Sabbath of the Lord in both the Old and New Testament.

CHAPTER 6

ROME'S CHALLENGE

February 24, 1893, the General Conference of Seventh-day Adventists adopted certain resolutions appealing to the government and people of the United States from the decision of the Supreme Court declaring this to be a Christian nation, and from the action of Congress in legislating upon the subject of religion, and the remonstrating against the principle and all the consequences of the same. In March, 1893, the International Religious Liberty Association printed these resolutions in a tract entitled *Appeal and Remonstrance.* On receipt of one of these, the editor of the *Catholic Mirror* of Baltimore, Maryland, published a series of four editorials, which appeared in that paper September 2, 9, 16, and 23, 1893. The *Catholic Mirror* was the official organ of Cardinal Gibbons and the Papacy in the United States. These articles, therefore, although not written by the Cardinal's own hand, appeared under his official sanction, and as the expression of the Papacy on this subject, are the open challenge of the Papacy to Protestantism, and the demand of the Papacy that Protestants shall render to the Papacy an account of why they keep Sunday and also of how they keep it. The following is a reprint of these editorials.

THE CHRISTIAN SABBATH
[From the Catholic Mirror of Sept. 2, 1893.]

The Genuine Offspring of the Union of the Holy Spirit and the Catholic Church His Spouse. The claims of Protestantism to Any Part Therein Proved to Be Groundless, Self-Contradictory, and Suicidal.

Our attention has been called to the above subject in the past week by the receipt of a brochure of twenty-one pages published by the International Religious Liberty Association entitled,

"Appeal and Remonstrance." embodying resolutions adopted by the General Conference of the Seventh-day Adventists (Feb. 24, 1893). The resolutions criticize and censure, with much acerbity, the action of the United States Congress, and of the Supreme Court, for invading the rights of the people by closing the World's Fair on Sunday.

The Adventists are the only body of Christians with the Bible as their teacher, who can find no warrant in its pages for the change of day from the seventh to the first. Hence their appellation, "Seventh-day Adventists". Their cardinal principle consists in setting apart Saturday for the exclusive worship of God, in conformity with the positive command of God Himself, repeatedly reiterated in the sacred books of the Old and New Testaments, literally obeyed by the children of Israel for thousands of years to this day and endorsed by the teaching and practice of the Son of God whilst on earth.

Per contra, the Protestants of the world, the Adventists excepted, with the same Bible as their cherished and sole infallible teacher, by their practice, since their appearance in the sixteenth century, with the time honored practice of the Jewish people before their eyes have rejected the day named for His worship by God and assumed in apparent contradiction of His command, a day for His worship never once referred to for that purpose, in the pages of that Sacred Volume.

What Protestant pulpit does not ring almost every Sunday with loud and impassioned invectives against Sabbath violation? Who can forget the fanatical clamor of the Protestant ministers throughout the length and breadth of the land against opening the gates of the World's Fair on Sunday? The thousands of petitions, signed by millions, to save the Lord's Day from desecration? Surely, such general and widespread excitement and noisy remonstrance could not have existed without the strongest grounds for such animated protests.

And when quarters were assigned at the World's Fair to the various sects of Protestantism for the exhibition of articles, who can forget the emphatic expression of virtuous and conscientious indignation exhibited by our Presbyterian brethren, as soon as they learned of the decision of the Supreme Court not to interfere in the Sunday opening? The newspapers informed us that they flatly refused to utilize the space accorded them, or open their boxes, demanding the right to withdraw the articles, in rigid adherence to their principles, and thus decline all contact with the sacrilegious and Sabbath-breaking Exhibition.

Doubtless, our Calvinistic brethren deserved and shared the sympathy of all the other sects, who, however, lost the opportunity of posing as martyrs in vindication of the Sabbath observance.

They thus became "a spectacle to the world, to angels, and to men," although their Protestant brethren, who failed to share the monopoly, were uncharitably and enviously disposed to attribute their steadfast adherence to religious principle, to Pharisaical pride and dogged obstinacy.

Our purpose in throwing off this article, is to shed such light on this all important question (for were the Sabbath question to be removed from the Protestant pulpit, the sects would feel lost, and the preachers be deprived of their "Cheshire cheese".) that our readers may be able to comprehend the question in all its bearings, and thus reach a clear conviction.

The Christian world is, morally speaking, united on the question and practice of worshiping God on the first day of the week.

The Israelites, scattered all over the earth, keep the last day of the week sacred to the worship of the Deity. In this particular, the Seventh-day Adventists (a sect of Christians numerically few) have also selected the same day.

Israelites and Adventists both appeal to the Bible for the divine command, persistently obliging the strict observance of Saturday.

The Israelite respects the authority of the Old Testament only, but the Adventist, who is a Christian, accepts the New Testament on the same ground as the Old: viz..an inspired record also. He finds that the Bible, his teacher, is consistent in both parts, that the Redeemer, during His mortal life, never kept any other day than Saturday. The gospels plainly evince to him this fact; whilst, in the pages of the Acts of the Apostles, the Epistles, and the Apocalypse, not the vestige of an act canceling the Saturday arrangement can be found.

The Adventists, therefore, in common with the Israelites, derive their belief from the Old Testament, which position is confirmed by the New Testament, endorsing fully by the life and practice of the Redeemer and His apostles the teaching of the Sacred Word for nearly a century of the Christian era.

Numerically considered, the Seventh-day Adventists form an insignificant portion of the Protestant population of the earth, but, as the question is not one of numbers, but of truth, fact, and right, a strict sense of justice forbids the condemnation of this little sect without a calm and unbiased investigation: this is none of our funeral.

The Protestant world has been, from its infancy, in the sixteenth century, in thorough accord with the Catholic Church, in keeping "holy," not Saturday, but Sunday. The discussion of the grounds that led to this unanimity of sentiment and practice for over 300 years must help toward placing Protestantism on a solid basis in this particular, should the arguments in favor of its position overcome those furnished by the Israelites and Adventists, the Bible, the sole recognized teacher of both litigants, being the umpire and witness. If, however, on the other hand, the latter furnish arguments, incontrovertible by the great mass of Protestants, both classes of litigants, appealing to their common teacher, the Bible, the great body of Protestants so far from clamoring, as they do with vigorous pertinacity for the strict keeping of Sunday, have no other recourse left than the admission that they have been teaching and practicing what is Scripturally false for over three centuries, by adopting the teaching and practice of the what they have always pretended to believe an apostate church, contrary to every warrant and teaching of sacred Scripture. To add to the intensity of this Scriptural and unpardonable blunder, it involves one of the most positive and emphatic commands of God to His servant, man: "Remember the Sabbath day, to keep it holy."

No Protestant living today has ever yet obeyed that command preferring to follow the apostate church referred to than his teacher, the Bible which from Genesis to Revelation, teaches no other doctrine, should the Israelites and Seventh-day Adventists be correct. Both sides appeal to the Bible as their "infallible" teacher. Let the Bible decide whether Saturday or Sunday be the day enjoined by God. One of the two bodies must be wrong, and , whereas a false position on this all-important question involves terrible penalties, threatened by God Himself, against the transgressor of this "perpetual covenant," we shall enter on the discussion of the merits of the arguments wielded by both sides. Neither is the discussion of this paramount subject above the capacity of ordinary minds, nor does it involve extraordinary study. It resolves itself into a few plain questions easy of solution:

1st. Which day of the week does the Bible enjoin to be kept holy?

2nd. Has the New Testament modified by precept or practice the original command?

3rd. Have Protestants, since the sixteenth century, obeyed the command of God by keeping "holy" the day enjoined by their infallible guide and teacher, the Bible? and if not, why not?

To the above three questions, we pledge ourselves to furnish as many intelligent answers, which cannot fail to vindicate the truth and uphold the deformity of error.

[From the Catholic Mirror of Sept. 9, 1893]
"But faith, fanatic faith, once wedded fast
To some dear falsehood, hugs it to the last"
         - Moore

Conformably to our promise in our last issue, we proceed to unmask one of the most flagrant errors and most unpardonable inconsistencies of the Biblical rule of faith. Lest, however, we be misunderstood, we deem it necessary to premise that

Protestantism recognizes no rule of faith, no teacher, save the "infallible Bible." As the Catholic yields his judgment in spiritual matters implicitly, and with unreserved confidence, to the voice of his church, so, too, the Protestant recognizes no teacher but the Bible. All his spirituality is derived from its teachings. It is to him the voice of God addressing him through his sole inspired teacher. It embodies his religion, his faith, and his practice. The language of Chillingworth, "The Bible, the whole Bible, and nothing but the Bible, is the religion of Protestants," is only one form of the same idea multifariously convertible into other forms, such as "the book of God," "the Charter of Our Salvation," "the Oracle of Our Christian Faith," "God's Text-Book to the race of Mankind," etc.,etc. It is, then, an incontrovertible fact that the Bible alone is the teacher of Protestant Christianity Assuming this fact, we will now proceed to discuss the merits of the question involved in our last issue.

Recognizing what is undeniable, the fact of a direct contradiction between the teaching and practice of Protestant Christianity --the Seventh-day Adventists excepted--on the one hand, and that of the Jewish people on the other, both observing different days of the week for the worship of God, we will proceed to take the testimony of the only available witness in the premises: viz., the testimony of the teacher common to both claimants, the Bible. The first expression with which we come in contact in the Sacred Word, is found in Genesis 2:2: "And on the seventh day He [God] rested from all His work which He had made." The next reference to this matter is to be found in Exodus 20, where God commanded the seventh day to be kept, because He had Himself rested from the work of creation on that day: and the sacred text informs us that for that reason He desired it kept, in the following words: "Wherefore, the Lord blessed the seventh day and sanctified it." Again, we read in chapter 31, verse 15: "Six days you shall do work: in the seventh day is the Sabbath, the rest holy to the Lord:" sixteenth verse: "It is an everlasting covenant," "and a perpetual sign," "for in six days the Lord made heaven and earth, and in the seventh He ceased from work."

In the Old Testament, reference is made on hundred and twenty-six times to the Sabbath, and all these texts conspire harmoniously in voicing the will of God commanding the seventh day to be kept, because God Himself first kept it, making it obligatory on all as "a perpetual covenant." Nor can we imagine any one foolhardy enough to question the identity of Saturday with the Sabbath or seventh day, seeing that the people of Israel have been keeping the Saturday from the giving of the law, A.M. 2514 to AD 1893, a period of 3383 years. with the example of the Israelites before our eyes today, there is no historical fact better established than that referred to: viz., that the chosen people of God, the guardians of the Old Testament, the living representatives of the only divine religion hitherto, had for a period of 1490 years anterior to Christianity, preserved by weekly practice the living tradition of the correct interpretation of the special day of the week, Saturday, to be kept "holy to the Lord," which tradition they have extended by their practice to an additional period of 1893 years more, thus covering the full extent of the Christian dispensation. We deem it necessary to be perfectly clear on this point, for reasons that will appear more fully hereafter. The Bible--Old Testament--confirmed by the living tradition of a weekly practice for 3383 years by the chosen people of God, teaches then, with absolute certainty, that God had, Himself, named the day to be "kept holy to Him,"--that the day was Saturday, and that any violation of that command was punishable with death. "Keep you My Sabbath, for it is holy unto you: he that shall profane it shall be put to death: he that shall do any work in it, his soul shall perish in the midst of his people." Ex.31:14.

It is impossible to realize a more severe penalty than that so solemnly uttered by God Himself in the above text, on all who violate a command referred to no less than one hundred and twenty-six times in the old law. The ten commandments of the Old Testament are formally impressed on the memory of the child of the Biblical Christian as soon as possible, but there is not one of the ten made more emphatically familiar, both in Sunday school and pulpit, than that of keeping "holy" the Sabbath day.

Having secured with absolute certainty the will of God as regards the day to be kept holy, from His Sacred word, because he rested on that day, which day is confirmed to us by the practice of His chosen people for thousands of years, we are naturally induced to inquire when and where God changed the day for His worship; for it is patent to the world that a change of day has taken place, and inasmuch as no indication of such change can be found within the pages of the Old Testament, nor in the practice of the Jewish people who continue for nearly nineteen centuries of Christianity obeying the written command, we must look to the exponent of the Christian dispensation: viz., the New Testament, for the command of God canceling the old Sabbath, Saturday.

We now approach a period covering little short of nineteen centuries, and proceed to investigate whether the supplemental divine teacher--the New Testament--contains a decree canceling the mandate of the old law, and, at the same time, substituting a day for the divinely instituted Sabbath of the old law. Viz. Saturday; for, inasmuch as Saturday was the day kept and ordered to be kept by God. Divine authority alone, under the form of a canceling decree, could abolish the Saturday covenant, and another divine mandate, appointing by name another day to be kept "holy," other than Saturday, is equally necessary to satisfy the conscience of the Christian believer. The Bible being the only teacher recognized by the Biblical Christian, the Old Testament failing to point out a change of day and yet another day than Saturday being kept "holy" by the Biblical world, it is surely incumbent on the reformed Christian to point out in the pages of the New Testament, the new divine decree repealing that of Saturday and substituting that of Sunday, kept by Biblicals since the dawn of the Reformation.

Examining the New Testament from cover to cover, critically, we find the Sabbath referred to sixty-one times. We find, too, that the Saviour invariably selected the Sabbath (Saturday) to teach in the synagogues and work miracles. The four Gospels refer to the Sabbath (Saturday) fifty-one times.

In one instance the Redeemer refers to Himself as "the Lord of the Sabbath," as mentioned by Matthew and Luke, but during the whole record of His life, whilst invariably keeping and utilizing the day (Saturday). He never once hinted at a desire to change it. His apostles and personal friends afford to us a striking instance of their scrupulous observance of it after His death, and, whilst His body was yet in the tomb, Luke (23:56) informs us: "And they returned and prepared spices and ointments and rested on the Sabbath day according to the commandment." "But on the first day of the week, very early in the morning, they came, bringing the spices they had prepared Good Friday evening, because the Sabbath drew near." Verse 54. This action on the part of the personal friends of the Saviour, proves beyond contradiction that after His death they kept "holy" the Saturday and regarded the Sunday as any other day of the week. Can anything, therefore, be more conclusive than that the apostles and the holy women never knew any Sabbath but Saturday, up to the day of Christ's death?

We now approach the investigation of this interesting question for the next thirty years, as narrated by the evangelist, St. Luke, in his Acts of the Apostles. Surely some vestige of the canceling act can be discovered in the practice of the apostles during that protracted period.

But alas! We are once more doomed to disappointment. Nine times do we find the Sabbath referred to in the Acts, but it is the Saturday (the Old Sabbath). Should our readers desire the proof, we refer them to chapter and verse in each instance. Acts 13:14, 27, 42, 44. Once more, Acts 15: 21; again, Acts 16: 13; 17:2; 18:4. "And he (Paul) reasoned in the synagogue every Sabbath, and persuaded the Jews and the Greeks." Thus the Sabbath (Saturday) from Genesis to Revelation!!! Thus, it is impossible to find in the New Testament the slightest interference by the Saviour or His apostles with the original Sabbath, but on the contrary, an entire acquiescence in the original arrangement;

nay, a plenary endorsement by Him, whilst living: and an unvaried, active participation in the keeping of that day and no other by the apostles for thirty years after His death, as the Acts of the Apostles has abundantly testified to us.

Hence the conclusion is inevitable: viz,. that of those who follow the Bible as their guide, the Israelites and Seventh-day Adventists have the exclusive weight of evidence on their side, whilst the Biblical Protestant has not a word in self-defense for his substitution of Sunday for Saturday. More anon.

[From the Catholic Mirror of Sept. 16, 1893.]

When his satanic majesty, who was "a murderer from the beginning." "and the father of lies," undertook to open the eyes of our first mother, Eve, by stimulating her ambition, "You shall be as gods, knowing good and evil" his action was but the first of many plausible and successful efforts employed later, in the seduction of millions of her children. Like Eve, they learn too late. Alas! the value of the inducements held out to allure her weak children from allegiance to God. Nor does the subject matter of this discussion form an exception to the usual tactics of his sable majesty.

Over three centuries since, he plausibly represented to a large number of discontented and ambitious Christians the bright prospect of the successful inauguration of a "new departure," by the abandonment of the Church instituted by the Son of God, as their teacher, and the assumption of a new teacher--the Bible alone--as their newly fledged oracle.

The sagacity of the evil one foresaw but the brilliant success of this maneuver. Nor did the result fall short of his most sanguine expectations.

A bold and adventurous spirit was alone needed to head the expedition. Him his satanic majesty soon found in the apostate monk, Luther, who himself repeatedly testifies to the close familiarity that existed between his master and himself, in his "Table Talk," and other works published in 1558, at Wittenberg, under the inspection of Melancthon. His colloquies with Satan on various occasions, are testified to by Luther himself--a witness worthy of all credibility. What the agency of the serpent tended so effectually to achieve in the garden, the agency of Luther achieved in the Christian world.

"Give them a pilot to their wandering fleet,
Bold in his art, and tutored to deceit:
Whose hand adventurous shall their helm misguide
To hostile shores, or'whelm them in the tide."

As the end proposed to himself by the evil one in his raid on the church of Christ was the destruction of Christianity, we are now engaged in sifting the means adopted by him to insure his success therein. So far, they have been found to be misleading, self-contradictory, and fallacious. We will now proceed with the further investigation of this imposture.

Having proved to a demonstration that the Redeemer, in no instance, had, during the period of His life, deviated from the faithful observance of the Sabbath (Saturday), referred to by the four evangelists fifty-one times, although He had designated Himself "Lord of the Sabbath," He never having once, by command or practice hinted at a desire on His part to change the day by the substitution of another and having called special attention to the conduct of the apostles and the holy women, the very evening of His death, securing beforehand spices and ointments to e used in embalming His body the morning after the Sabbath (Saturday) as St. Luke so clearly informs us (Luke 24:1), thereby placing beyond peradventure, the divine action and will of the son of God during life by keeping the Sabbath steadfastly; and having called attention to the action of His living representatives after His death, as proved by St. Luke, having also placed before our readers the indisputable fact that the apostles for the following thirty years (Acts) never deviated from the practice of their divine Master in this particular, as St. Luke , Acts 18:1) assures us: "And he [Paul] reasoned in the synagogues every Sabbath (Saturday, and persuaded the Jews and the Greeks." The Gentile converts were, as we see from the text, equally instructed with the Jews, to keep the Saturday, having been converted to Christianity on that day, "the Jews and the Greeks" collectively.

Having also called attention to the texts of the Acts bearing on the exclusive use of the Sabbath by the Jews and Christians for thirty years after the death of the Saviour as the only day of the week observed by Christ and His apostles, which period exhausts the inspired record, we now proceed to supplement our proofs that the Sabbath (Saturday) enjoyed this exclusive privilege, by calling attention to every instance wherein the sacred record refers to the first day of the week.

The first reference to Sunday after the resurrection of Christ is to be found in St. Luke's gospel, chapter 24, verses 33-40, and St. John 20:19.

The above texts themselves refer to the sole motive of this gathering on the part of the apostles. It took place on the day of the resurrection (Easter Sunday), not for the purpose of inaugurating "the new departure" from the old Sabbath (Saturday) by keeping "holy" the new day, for there is not a hint given of prayer, exhortation, or the reading of the Scriptures, but it indicates the utter demoralization of the apostles by informing mankind that they were huddled together in that room in Jerusalem "for fear of the Jews", as St. John, quoted above, plainly informs us.

The second reference to Sunday is to be found in St. John's Gospel, 20th chapter, 26th to 29th verses: "And after eight days, the disciples were again within, and Thomas with them." The resurrected Redeemer availed Himself of this meeting of all the apostles to confound the incredulity of Thomas, who had been absent from the gathering on Easter Sunday evening. This would have furnished a golden opportunity to the Redeemer to change the day in the presence of all His apostles, but we state the simple fact that, on this occasion, as on Easter day, not q word is said of prayer, praise, or reading of the Scriptures.

The third instance on record, wherein the apostles were assembled on Sunday, is to be found in Acts 2:1; "The apostles were all of one accord in one place." (Feast of Pentecost--Sunday) Now, will this text afford to our Biblical Christian brethren a vestige of hope that Sunday substitutes, at length, Saturday? For when we inform them that the Jews had been keeping this Sunday for 1500 years and have been keeping it for eighteen centuries after the establishment of Christianity, at the same time keeping the weekly Sabbath, there is not to be found either consolation or comfort in this text. Pentecost is the fiftieth day after the Passover, which was called the Sabbath of weeks consisting of seven times seven days and the day after the completion of the seventh weekly Sabbath day, was the chief day of the entire festival, necessarily Sunday. What Israelite would not pity the cause that would seek to discover the origin of the keeping of the first day of the week in his festival of Pentecost, that has been kept by him yearly for over 3,000 years? Who but the Biblical Christians, driven to the wall for a pretext to excuse his sacrilegious desecration of the Sabbath, always kept by Christ and His apostles would have resorted to the Jewish festival of Pentecost for his act of rebellion against his God and his teacher, the Bible.

Once more, the Biblical apologists for the change of day call our attention to the Acts, chapter 20, verses 6 and 7; "And upon the first day of the week, when the disciples came together to break bread." etc. To all appearances the above text should furnish some consolation to our disgruntled Biblical friends, but being a Marplot, we cannot allow them even this crumb of comfort. We reply by the axiom: "Quod probat nimis, probat nihil"--"What proves too much, proves nothing." Let us call attention to the same, Acts 2:46; "And they, continuing daily in the temple, and breaking bread from house to house," etc. Who does not see at a glance that the text produced to prove the exclusive prerogative of Sunday, vanishes into thin air--an ignis fatuus--when placed in juxtaposition with the 46th verse of the same chapter? What the Biblical Christian claims by this text for

Sunday alone the same authority, St. Luke, informs us was common to every day of the week; "and they, continuing daily in the temple, and breaking bread from house to house."

One text more presents itself, apparently leaning toward a substitution of Sunday for Saturday. It is taken from St. Paul, I Cor. 16:1,2; "Now concerning the collection for the saints." "On the first day of the week, let every one of you lay by him in store," etc. Presuming that the request of St. Paul had been strictly attended to, let us call attention to what had been done each Saturday during the Saviour's life and continued for thirty years after, as the book of Acts informs us.

The followers of the Master met "every Sabbath" to hear the word of God; the scriptures were read "every Sabbath day." "And Paul, as his manner was to reason in the synagogue every Sabbath, interposing the name of the Lord Jesus," etc. Acts 18:4. What more absurd conclusion than to infer that reading of the Scriptures, prayer, exhortation and preaching, which formed the routine duties of every Saturday, as has been abundantly proved, were overslaughed by a request to take up a collection on another day of the week?

In order to appreciate fully the value of this text now under consideration, it is only needful to recall the action of the apostles and holy women on Good Friday before sundown. They bought the spices and ointments after He was taken down from the cross; they suspended all action until the Sabbath "holy to the Lord" had pass, and then took steps on Sunday morning to complete the process of embalming the sacred body of Jesus.

Why, may we ask, did they not proceed to complete the work of embalming on Saturday?--Because they knew well that the embalming of the sacred body of their Master would interfere with the strict observance of the Sabbath, the keeping of which was paramount; and until it can be shown that the Sabbath day immediately preceding the Sunday of our text had not been kept (which would be false, inasmuch as every Sabbath had been kept), the request of St. Paul to make the collection on Sunday remains to be classified with the work of the embalming of

Christ's body, which could not be effected on the Sabbath, and was consequently deferred to the next convenient day: viz. Sunday, or the first day of the week.

Having disposed of every text to be found in the New Testament referring to the Sabbath (Saturday), and to the first day of the week (Sunday); and having shown conclusively from these texts, that, so far, not a shadow of pretext can be found in the Sacred Volume for the Biblical substitution of Sunday for Saturday; it only remains for us to investigate the meaning of the expressions "Lord's Day," and "day of the Lord," to be found in the New Testament, which we propose to do in our next article, and conclude with apposite remarks on the incongruities of a system of religion which we shall have proved to be indefensible, self-contradictory, and suicidal.

[From the Catholic Mirror of Sept. 23, 1893.]

"Halting on crutches of unequal size.
One leg by truth supported, one by lies,
Thus sidle to the goal with awkward pace,
Secure of nothing but to lose the race."

In the present article we propose to investigate carefully a new (and the last) class of proof assumed to convince the biblical Christian that God had substituted Sunday for Saturday for His worship in the new law, and that the divine will is to be found recorded by the Holy Ghost in apostolic writings.

We are informed that this radical change has found expression, over and over again, in a series of texts in which the expression, "the day of the Lord," or "the Lord's day," is to be found.

The class of texts in the New Testament, under the title "Sabbath," numbering sixty-one in the Gospels, Acts, and Epistles; and the second class, in which "the first day of the week," or Sunday, having been critically examined (the latter class numbering nine [eight]); and having been found not to afford the slightest clue to a change of will on the part of God as to His day of worship by man, we now proceed to examine the third and last class of texts relied on to save the Biblical system from the arraignment of seeking to palm off on the world, in the name of God a decree for which there is not the slightest warrant or authority from their teacher, the Bible.

The first text of this class is to be found in the Acts of the Apostles 2:20: "The sun shall be turned into darkness, and the moon into blood, before that great and notable day of the Lord shall come." How many Sundays have rolled by since that prophecy was spoken? So much for that effort to pervert the meaning of the sacred text from the judgment day to Sunday!

The second text of this class is to be found in I Cor. 1:8; "Who shall also confirm you unto the end. That you may be blameless in the day of our Lord Jesus Christ." What simpleton does not see that the apostle here plainly indicates the day of judgment? The next text of this class that presents itself is to be found in the same Epistle, chapter 5:5; "To deliver such a one to Satan for the destruction of the flesh, that the spirit may be saved in the day of the Lord Jesus." The incestuous Corinthian was, of course, saved on the Sunday next following!! How pitiable such a makeshift as this! The fourth text, 2 Cor. 1:13,14; "And I trust ye shall acknowledge even to the end, even as ye also are ours in the day of our Lord Jesus."

Sunday, or the day of judgment, which? The fifth text is from St. Paul to the Philippians, chapter 1, verse 6: "Being confident of this very thing, that He who hath begun a good work in you, will perfect it until the day of Jesus Christ." The good people of Philippi, in attaining perfection on the following Sunday, could afford to laugh at our modern rapid transit!

We beg leave to submit our sixth of the class; viz. Philippians, first chapter, tenth verse: "That he may be sincere without offense unto the day of Christ." That day was next Sunday, forsooth! not so long to wait after all. The seventh text, 2 Peter 3:10; "But the day of the Lord will come as a thief in the night." The application of this text to Sunday passes the bounds of absurdity.

The eighth text, 2 Peter 3:12; "Waiting for and hastening unto the coming of the day of the Lord, by which the heavens being on fire, shall be dissolved." etc. This day of the Lord is the same referred to in the previous text, the application of both of which to Sunday next would have left the Christian world sleepless the next Saturday night.

We have presented to our readers eight of the nine texts relied on to bolster up by text of Scripture the sacrilegious effort to palm off the "Lord's day" for Sunday, and with what result? Each furnishes prima facie evidence of the last day, referring to it directly, absolutely, and unequivocally.

The ninth text wherein we meet the expression "the Lord's day," is the last to be found in the apostolic writings. The Apocalypse, or Revelation, chapter 1:10, furnishes it in the following words of St. John: "I was in the Spirit on the Lord's day;" but it will afford no more comfort to our Biblical friends than its predecessors of the same series. Has St. John used the expression previously in his Gospel or Epistles?--Emphatically, No. Has he had occasion to refer to Sunday hitherto?--Yes, twice. How did he designate Sunday on these occasions? Easter Sunday was called by him (John 20:1) "The first day of the week."

Again, chapter twenty, nineteenth verse: "Now when it was late that same day, being the first day of the week." Evidently, although inspired, both in his gospel and Epistles, he called Sunday "the first day of the week." On what grounds then, can it be assumed that he dropped that designation? Was he more inspired when he wrote the apocalypse, or did he adopt a new title for Sunday because it was now in vogue?

A reply to these questions would be supererogatory especially to the latter, seeing that the same expression had been used eight times already by St. Luke, St. Paul, and St. Peter, all under divine inspiration and surely the Holy spirit would not inspire St. John to call Sunday the Lord's day whilst He inspired St. Luke, Paul, and Peter, collectively, to entitle the day of judgment "the Lord's day." Dialecticians reckon amongst the infallible motives of certitude, the moral motive of analogy or induction, by which we are enabled to conclude with certainty from the known to the unknown being absolutely certain of the meaning of an expression uttered eight times, we conclude that the same expression can have only the same meaning when uttered the ninth time, especially when we know that on the nine occasions the expressions were inspired by the Holy Spirit.

Nor are the strongest intrinsic grounds wanting to prove that this like its sister texts, contains the same meaning, St. John (Rev. 1:10) says: "I was in the Spirit on the Lord's day;" but he furnishes us the key to this expression, chapter four, first and second verses; "After this I looked and behold a door was opened in heaven." A voice said to him; "Come up hither, and I will show you the things which must be hereafter," Let us ascend in spirit with John. Whither?--through that "door in heaven," to heaven. a And what shall we see?--"The things that must be hereafter," Chapter four, first verse. He ascended in spirit to heaven. He was ordered to write, in full, his vision of what is to take place antecedent to and concomitantly with, "the Lord's day," or the day of judgment; the expression "Lords day" being confined in Scripture to the day of judgment, exclusively.

We have studiously and accurately collected from the New Testament every available proof that could be adduced in favor of a law canceling the Sabbath day of the old law, or one substituting another day for the Christian dispensation. We have been careful to make the above distinction, lest it might be advanced that the third (in the Catholic enumeration the Sabbath commandment is the third of the commandments) commandment was abrogated under the new law. Any such plea has been overruled by the action of the Methodist Episcopal bishops in their pastoral 1874, and quoted by the *New Your Herald* of the same date, of the following tenor; "The Sabbath instituted in the beginning and confirmed again and again by Moses and the prophets, has never been abrogated. A part of the moral law, not a part or tittle of its sanctity has been taken away." The above official pronunciamento has committed that large body of

Biblical Christians to the permanence of the third commandment under the new law.

We again beg leave to call the special attention of our readers to the twentieth of "the thirty-nine articles of religion" of the Book of Common Prayer: "It is not lawful for the church to ordain anything that is contrary to God's written word"

CONCLUSION

We have in this series of articles, taken much pains for the instruction of our readers to prepare them by presenting a number of undeniable facts found in the word of God to arrive at a conclusion absolutely irrefragable. When the Biblical system put in an appearance in the sixteenth century, it not only seized on the temporal possessions of the Church, but in its vandalic crusade stripped Christianity, as far as it could, of all the sacraments instituted by its Founder, of the holy sacrifice, etc., etc., retaining nothing but the Bible, which its exponents pronounced their sole teacher in Christian doctrine and morals.

Chief amongst their articles of belief was, and is today, the permanent necessity of keeping the Sabbath holy. In fact, it has been for the past 300 years the only article of the Christian belief in which there has been a plenary consensus of Biblical representatives. The keeping of the Sabbath constitutes the sum and substance of the Biblical theory. The pulpits resound weekly with incessant tirades against the lax manner of keeping the Sabbath in Catholic countries as contrasted with the proper, Christian, self-satisfied mode of keeping the day in Biblical countries. Who can ever forget the virtuous indignation manifested by the Biblical preachers throughout the length and breadth of our country, from every Protestant pulpit as long as the question of opening the World's Fair on Sunday was yet undecided; and who does not know today, that one sect, to mark its holy indignation at the decision, has never yet opened the boxes that contained its articles at the World's Fair?

These superlatively good and unctuous Christians, by conning over their bible carefully, can find their counterpart in a certain class of unco-good people in the days of the Redeemer, who haunted Him night and day, distressed beyond measure, and scandalized beyond forbearance, because He did not keep the Sabbath in as straight -laced manner as themselves.

They hated Him for using common sense in reference to the day, and He found no epithets expressive enough of His supreme contempt for their Pharisaical pride. And it is very probable that the divine mind has not modified its views today anent the blatant outcry of their followers and sympathizers at the close of this nineteenth century. But when we add to all this the fact that whilst the Pharisees of old kept the true Sabbath, our modern Pharisees, counting on the credulity and simplicity of their dupes, have never once in their lives kept the true Sabbath which their divine Master kept to His dying day and which His apostles kept, after His example, for thirty years afterward according to the Sacred Record, the most glaring contradiction involving a deliberate sacrilegious rejection of a most positive precept is presented to us today in the action of the Biblical Christian world. The Bible and the Sabbath constitute the watchword of Protestantism: but we have demonstrated that it is the Bible against their Sabbath. We have shown that no greater contradiction ever existed than their theory and practice. We have proved that neither their biblical ancestors nor themselves have ever kept one Sabbath day in their lives.

The Israelites and Seventh-day Adventists are witnesses of their weekly desecration of the day named by God so repeatedly, and whilst they have ignored and condemned their teacher, the bible, they have adopted a day kept by the Catholic Church. What Protestant can, after perusing these articles, with a clear conscience, continue to disobey the command of God enjoining Saturday to be kept which command his teacher, the Bible, from Genesis to Revelation, records as the will of God?

The history of the world cannot present a more stupid, self-stultifying specimen of dereliction of principle than this. The teacher demands emphatically in every page that the law of the Sabbath be observed every week, by all recognizing it as "the only infallible teacher," whilst the disciples of that teacher have not once for over three hundred years observed the divine precept! That immense concourse of Biblical Christians, the Methodists, have declared that the Sabbath has never been abrogated, whilst the followers of the Church of England, together with her daughter, the Episcopal Church of the United States, are committed by the twentieth article of religion, already quoted, to the ordinance that the Church cannot lawfully ordain anything "contrary to God's written word." god's written word enjoins His worship to be observed on Saturday absolutely, repeatedly, and most emphatically, with a most positive threat of death to him who disobeys. All the Biblical sects occupy the same self-stultifying position which no explanation can modify, much less justify.

How truly do the words of the Holy Spirit apply to this deplorable situation! "Iniquitas mentita est sibi"- "Iniquity hath lied to itself." Proposing to follow the Bible only as a teacher, yet before the world, the sole teacher is ignominiously thrust aside, and the teaching and practice of the Catholic Church - "the mother of abominations," when it suits their purpose so to designate her - adopted, despite the most terrible threats pronounced by God Himself against those who disobey the command, "Remember to keep holy the Sabbath."

Before closing this series of articles, we beg to call the attention of our readers once more to our caption, introductory of each; vis., 1. The Christian Sabbath, the genuine offspring of the union of the Holy Spirit with the Catholic Church His spouse. 2. The claim of Protestantism to any part therein proved to be groundless, self-contradictory and suicidal.

The first proposition needs little proof. The Catholic Church for over one thousand years before the existence of a Protestant, by virtue of her divine mission, changed the day from Saturday to Sunday. We say by virtue of her divine mission, because He who called Himself the "Lord of the Sabbath," endowed her with His own power to teach, "He that heareth you, heareth me;" commanded all who believe in Him to hear her, under penalty of being placed with the "heathen and publican;" and promised to be with her to the end of the world. She holds her charter as the teacher from him- a charter as infallible as perpetual. The Protestant world at its birth found the Christian Sabbath too strongly entrenched to run counter to its existence; it was therefore placed under the necessity of acquiescing in the arrangement, thus implying the Church's right to change the day, for over three hundred years. The Christian Sabbath is therefore to this day, the acknowledged offspring of the Catholic Church as spouse of the holy Ghost without a word of remonstrance from the Protestant world.

Let us now, however, take a glance at our second proposition, with the Bible alone as the teacher most emphatically forbids any change in the day for paramount reasons. The command calls for a "perpetual covenant." The day commanded to be kept by the teacher has never once been kept. Thereby developing an apostasy from an assumedly fixed principle, as self-contradictory, self-stultifying, and consequently as suicidal as it is within the power of language to express.

Nor are the limits of demoralization yet reached. Far from it. Their pretense for leaving the bosom if the Catholic Church was for apostasy from the truth as taught in the written word. They adopted the written word as their sole teacher, which they had no sooner done than they abandoned it promptly, as these articles have abundantly proved; and by a perversity as willful as erroneous, they accept the teaching of the Catholic Church in direct opposition to the plain, unvaried, and constant teaching of their sole teacher in the most essential doctrine of their religion, thereby emphasizing the situation in what may be aptly designated "a mockery, a delusion, and a snare."

[Editor's note--It was upon this very point that the Reformation was condemned by the Council of Trent. The Reformers had constantly charged, as here stated that the Catholic Church had apostatized from the truth as contained in the written word. "The written word," "The Bible and the Bible only," "Thus saith the Lord," these were their constant watchwords; and "The Scripture as in the written word the sole standard of appeal." This was the proclaimed platform of the Reformation and of Protestantism. "The Scripture and tradition." "The bible as interpreted by the Church and according to the unanimous consent of the fathers." This was the position and claim of the Catholic Church. This was the main issue in the Council of Trent, which was called especially to consider the questions that had been raised and forced upon the attention of Europe by the Reformers. The very first question concerning faith that was considered by the council was the question involved in this issue. There was a strong party even of the Catholics within the council who were in favor of abandoning tradition and adopting the Scriptures only, as the standard of authority. This view was so decidedly held in the debates in the council that the pope's legates actually wrote to him that there was "as strong tendency to set aside tradition altogether and to make Scripture the sole standard of appeal." But to do this would manifestly be to go a long way toward justifying the claim of the Protestants. By this crisis there was developed upon the ultra-Catholic portion of the council the task of convincing the others that "Scripture and tradition" were the only sure ground to stand upon. If this could be done, the council could be carried to issue a decree condemning the Reformation, otherwise not. The question was debated day after day, until the council was fairly brought to a standstill. Finally, after a long and intensive mental strain, the Archbishop of Reggio came into the council with substantially the following argument to the party who held for scripture alone:

"The Protestants claim to stand upon the written word only. They profess to hold the Scripture alone as the standard of faith. They justify their revolt by the plea that the Church has apostatized from the written word and follows tradition. Now the Protestant's claim, that they stand upon the written word only is not true. Their profession of holding the Scripture alone as the standard of faith, is false. PROOF: The written word explicitly enjoins the observance of the seventh day as the Sabbath. They do not observe the seventh day, but reject it. If they do truly hold the Scripture alone as their standard, they would be observing the seventh day as is enjoined in the scripture throughout. Yet they not only reject the observance of the Sabbath enjoined in the written word, but they have adopted and do practice the observance of Sunday, for which they have only the tradition of the Church. Consequently the claim of "Scripture alone as the standard.' fails; and the doctrine of "Scripture and tradition" as essential, is fully established, the Protestants themselves being judges."

There was no getting around this, for the Protestants own statement of faith--the Augsburg Confession 1530--had clearly admitted that "the observation of the Lord's day" had been appointed by "the Church" only.

The argument was hailed in the council as of Inspiration only; the party for "Scripture alone," surrendered; and the council at once unanimously condemned Protestantism and the whole Reformation as only an unwarranted revolt from the communion and authority of the Catholic Church; and proceeded, April 8, 1546 "to the promulgation of two decrees, the first of which enacts, under anathema, that Scripture and tradition are to be received and venerated equally, and that the deutero-canonical {the apocryphal} books are part of the cannon of Scripture. The second decree declares the Vulgate to be the sole authentic and standard Latin version, and gives it such authority as to supersede the original tests; forbids the interpretation of Scripture contrary to the sense received by the Church, "or even contrary to the unanimous consent of the Fathers," etc.

Thus it was the inconsistency of the Protestant practice with the Protestant profession that gave to the Catholic Church her long-sought and anxiously desired ground upon which to condemn Protestantism and the whole Reformation movement as only a selfishly ambitious rebellion against church authority. And in this vital controversy the key, the chiefest and culminative expression, of the Protestant inconsistency was in the rejection of the Sabbath of the Lord, the seventh day, enjoined in the Scriptures and the adoption and observance of the Sunday as enjoined by the Catholic Church.

And this is today the position of the respective parties to this controversy. Today, as this document shows, this is the vital issue upon which the Catholic Church arraigns Protestantism, and upon which she condemns the course of popular Protestantism as being "indefensible, self-contradictory, and suicidal," What will these Protestants, what will this Protestantism, do?]

Should any of the reverend parsons, who are habituated to howl so vociferously over every real or assumed desecration of that pious fraud, the Bible Sabbath, think well of entering a protest against our logical and Scriptural dissection of their mongrel pet, we can promise them that any reasonable attempt on their part to gather up the disjectamembra of the hybrid, and to restore to it a galvanized existence, will be met with genuine cordiality and respectful consideration on our part.

But we can assure our readers that we know these reverend howlers too well to expect a solitary bark from them in this instance. And they know us too well to subject themselves to the mortification which a further dissection of this antiscriptural question would necessarily entail. Their policy now is to "lay low" and they are sure to adopt it.

APPENDIX I

These articles are reprinted, and this leaflet is sent forth by the publishers, because it gives from and undeniable source and in no uncertain tone, the latest phase of the Sunday-observance controversy, which is now, and which indeed for some time has been, not only a national question, with leading nations, but also an international question. Not that we are glad to have it so; we would that it were far otherwise. We would that Protestants everywhere were so thoroughly consistent in profession and practice that there could be no possible room for the relations between them and Rome ever to take the shape which they have no taken.

But the situation in this matter is now as it is herein set forth. There is no escaping this fact. It therefore becomes the duty of the International religious Liberty Association to make known as widely as possible the true phase of this great question as it now stands. Not because we are pleased to have it so, but because it is so, whatever we or anybody else would or would not be pleased to have.

It is true that we have been looking for years for this question to assume precisely that attitude which it has now assumed, and which it so plainly set forth in this leaflet. We have told the people repeatedly, and Protestants especially, and yet more especially have we told those who were advocating Sunday laws and the recognition and legal establishment of Sunday by the United States, that in the course that was being pursued they were playing directly into the hands of Rome, and that as certainly as they succeeded, they would inevitably be called upon by Rome and Rome in possession of power too, to render to her an account as to why Sunday should be kept. This, we have told the people for years, would surely come. And now that it has come, it is only our duty to make it known as widely as it lies in our power to do.

It may be asked, Why did not Rome come out as boldly as this before? Why did she wait so long? It was not for her interest to do so before. When she should move, she desired to move with power, and power as yet she did not have. But in their strenuous efforts for the national governmental recognition and establishment of Sunday, the Protestants of the United States were doing more for her than she could possibly do for herself in the way of getting governmental power in her hands. This she well knew, and therefore only waited. And now that the Protestants, in alliance with her, have accomplished this awful thing, she at once rises up in all her native arrogance and old-time spirit, and calls upon the Protestants to answer to her for their observance of Sunday. This, too, she does because she is secure in the power which the Protestants have so blindly placed in her hands. In other words, the power which the Protestants have thus put into her hands she will now use to their destruction. Is any other evidence needed to show that the Catholic Mirror (Which means the Cardinal and the Catholic Church in America) has been waiting for this, than that furnished on page 21 of this leaflet? Please turn pack and look at that page and see the quotation clipped from the New York Herald in 1874, and which is now brought forth thus. Does not this show plainly that that statement of the Methodist bishops, just such a time as this? And more than this, the Protestants will find more such things which have been so laid up, and which will yet be used in a way that will both surprise and confound them.

This at present is a controversy between the Catholic Church and Protestants. As such only do we reproduce these editorials of the Catholic Mirror. The points controverted are points which are claimed by Protestants as in their favor. The argument is made by the Catholic Church; the answer devolves upon those Protestants who observe Sunday, not upon us. We can truly say, " This is none of our funeral." If they do not answer, she will make their silence their confession that is right, and she will use that against them accordingly. If they do answer she will use against them their own words, and as occasion may demand, the power which they have put into her hands. So that, so far as she is concerned, whether the Protestants answer or not, it is all the same. And how she looks upon them, and the spirit in which she proposes to deal with them henceforth is clearly manifested in the challenge made in the last paragraph of the reprint articles.

There is just one refuge left for the Protestants. That is to take their stand squarely and fully upon "the written word only," "the Bible and the Bible alone," and thus upon the Sabbath of the Lord. Thus acknowledging no authority but God's, wearing no sigh but His (Eze. 20: 12, 20), obeying His command, and shielded by His power, they shall have the victory over Rome and all her alliances, and stand upon the sea of glass, bearing the harps of God , with which their triumph shall be forever celebrated. (Revelation 18, and 15:2-4)

It is not yet too late for Protestants to redeem themselves. Will they do it? Will they stand consistently upon the Protestant profession? Or will they still continue to occupy the "indefensible, self-contradictory, and suicidal position of professing to be Protestants, yet standing on Catholic ground, receiving Catholic insult, and bearing Catholic condemnation? Will they indeed take the written word only, the Scripture alone, as their sole authority and their sole standard? Or will they still hold the "indefensible, self-contradictory, and suicidal "doctrine and practice of following the authority of the Catholic Church and of wearing the sign of her authority? Will they keep the Sabbath of the Lord, the seventh day, according to Scripture? or will they keep the Sunday according to the tradition of the Catholic Church?

Dear reader, which will you do?

APPENDIX II

Since the first edition of this publication was printed, the following appeared in an editorial in the Catholic Mirror in Dec. 23, 1893:

"The avidity with which these editorials have been sought, and the appearance of a reprint of them by the International Religious Liberty Association, published in Chicago, entitled, 'Rome's Challenge: Why Do Protestants Keep Sunday?' and offered for sale in Chicago, New York, California, Tennessee, London, Australia, Cape Town, Africa, and Ontario, Canada, together with the continuous demand, have prompted the Mirror to give permanent form to them, and thus comply with the demand.

"The pages of this brochure unfold to the reader one of the most glaringly conceivable contradictions existing between the practice and theory of the Protestant world, and unsusceptible of any rational solution, the theory claiming the Bible alone as the teacher, which unequivocally and most positively commands

Saturday to be kept 'holy,' whilst their practice proves that they utterly ignore the unequivocal requirements of their teacher, the Bible, and occupying Catholic ground for three centuries and a half, by abandonment of their theory, they stand before the world today the representatives of a system the most indefensible, self-contradictory, and suicidal that can be imagined.

"We feel that we cannot interest our readers more than to produce the 'Appendix' which the International Religious Liberty Association, an ultra-Protestant organization, has added to the reprint of our articles. The perusal of the Appendix will confirm the fact that our argument is unanswerable, and that to retire from Catholic territory where they have is either to retire from Catholic territory where they have been squatting for three centuries and a half, and accepting their own teacher, the Bible, in good faith, as so clearly suggested by the writer of the 'Appendix,' commence forthwith to keep the Saturday, the day enjoined by the Bible from Genesis to Revelation; or, abandoning the Bible as their sole teacher, cease to be squatters, and a living contradiction of their own principles, and taking out letters of adoption as citizens of the kingdom of Christ on earth - His Church - be no longer victims of self-delusive and necessary self-contradiction.

"The arguments contained in this pamphlet are firmly grounded on the word of God, and having been closely studied with the Bible in hand, leave no escape for the conscientious Protestant except the abandonment of Sunday worship and the return to Saturday, commanded by their teacher, the Bible, or, unwilling to abandon the tradition of the Catholic Church, which enjoins the keeping of Sunday, and which they have accepted in direct opposition to their teacher, the Bible, consistently accept her in all her teachings. Reason and common sense demand the acceptance of one or the other of these alternatives: either Protestantism and the keeping holy of Saturday, or Catholicity and the keeping of Sunday. Compromise is impossible."

CHAPTER 7

STUDY HELPS

DOES THIS VERSE SAY WHICH DAY IS THE LORD'S?
I was in the Spirit on the *Lord's day*, and heard behind me a great voice, as of a trumpet. *Revelation 1:10*

WHICH DAY DOES JESUS SAY IS HIS DAY?
Therefore the Son of man is Lord also of *the sabbath*. *Mark 2:28*

WHAT DID GOD CALL THE SABBATH?
If thou turn away thy foot from the sabbath, from doing thy pleasure on *my holy day*; and call the sabbath a delight, the holy of the LORD, honourable; and shalt honour him, not doing thine own ways, nor finding thine own pleasure, nor speaking thine own words: *Isaiah 58:13*

WHICH DAY IS THE BIBLE SABBATH?
Remember the sabbath day, to keep it holy.
Six days shalt thou labour, and do all thy work:
But *the seventh day is the sabbath of the LORD thy God*: in it thou shalt not do any work, thou, nor thy son, nor thy daughter, thy manservant, nor thy maidservant, nor thy cattle, nor thy stranger that is within thy gates:
For in six days the LORD made heaven and earth, the sea, and all that in them is, and rested the seventh day: wherefore the LORD blessed the sabbath day, and hallowed it. *Exodus 20:8-11*

WHEN WAS THE SABBATH MADE HOLY AND SANCTIFIED?
Thus the heavens and the earth were finished, and all the host of them.
And *on the seventh day God ended his work which he had*

made; and he rested on the seventh day from all his work which he had made. And *God blessed the seventh day, and sanctified it*: because that in ithe had rested from all his work which God created and made. *Genesis 2:1-3*

CAN WE KNOW FOR CERTAIN WHICH DAY IS THE SABBATH?
This man went unto Pilate, and begged the body of Jesus.
And he took it down, and wrapped it in linen, and laid it in a sepulchre that was hewn in stone, wherein never man before was laid. And that day was the preparation [Good Friday], and *the sabbath drew on.*
And the women also, which came with him from Galilee, followed after, and beheld the sepulchre, and how his body was laid.
And they returned, and prepared spices and ointments; and *rested the sabbath day according to the commandment.*
Now upon the first day [Easter Sunday] of the week, very early in the morning, they came unto the sepulchre, bringing the spices which they had prepared, and certain others with them. *Luke 23:52-24:1*
> NOTE: The Sabbath is the day between Good Friday and Easter Sunday, or Saturday, the seventh day of the week.

WAS THE SABBATH MADE FOR JUST THE JEWS?
And he said unto them, *The sabbath was made for man*, and not man for the sabbath: *Mark 2:27*
> NOTE: Abraham (the Father of the Jews) was not even born until more than 2,000 years after creation.

DID JESUS KEEP THE SABBATH COMMANDMENT?
And he came to Nazareth, where he had been brought up: and, *as his custom was,* he went into the synagogue *on the sabbath day*, and stood up for to read. *Luke 4:16*

DID PAUL KEEP THE BIBLE SABBATH?

And Paul, *as his manner was*, went in unto them, and *three sabbath days* reasoned with them out of the scriptures, *Acts 17:2*

DID GENTILE [NON-JEW] CHRISTIANS KEEP THE SABBATH?

And when the Jews were gone out of the synagogue, the *Gentiles besought that these words might be preached to them the next sabbath. Acts 13:42*

HOW MANY WERE KEEPING THE SABBATH?

And *the next sabbath day came almost the whole city together* to hear the word of God. *Acts 13:44*

WHEN DID THE APOSTLES MEET WITH THE WOMEN?

And *on the sabbath* we went out of the city by a river side, where prayer was wont to be made; and we sat down, and spake unto the women which resorted thither. *Acts 16:13*

HOW OFTEN DID EARLY CHRISTIANS MEET ON SABBATH?

And he reasoned in the synagogue *every sabbath*, and persuaded the Jews and the Greeks. *Acts 18:4*

WHAT DID JESUS SAY PRAY FOR 40 YEARS IN THE FUTURE?

But *pray ye that your flight be not* in the winter, neither *on the sabbath day. Matthew 24:20*

DID JESUS CHANGE ANY OF THE TEN COMMANDMENTS?

Think not that I am come to destroy the law, or the prophets: *I am not come to destroy*, but to fulfil.

For verily I say unto you, Till heaven and earth pass, *one jot or one tittle shall in no wise pass from the law,* till all be fulfilled. *Matthew 5:17, 18*

ARE GOD'S PEOPLE TO CONTINUE KEEPING THE SABBATH?

For we which have believed do enter into rest, as he said, As I have sworn in my wrath, if *they shall enter into my rest*: although the works were finished from the foundation of the world.

For *he spake* in a certain place *of the seventh day on this wise, And God did rest the seventh day from all his works...*

There remaineth therefore a rest to the people of God.

For he that is entered into his rest, he also hath ceased from his own works, as God did from his.

Let us labour therefore to *enter into that rest*, lest any man fall after the same example of unbelief. *Hebrews 4:3, 4, 9-11*

WHAT WORD SHOWS MAN WOULD FORGET THE SABBATH

Remember the sabbath day, to keep it holy. *Exodus 20:8*

WILL THE SABBATH BE KEPT IN THE NEW EARTH?

For as the new heavens and the new earth, which I will make, shall remain before me, saith the LORD, so shall your seed and your name remain.

And it shall come to pass, that from one new moon to another, and from one *sabbath* to another, *shall all flesh come to worship* before me, saith the LORD. *Isaiah 66:22, 23*

THE SABBATH IS TO BE A SIGN BETWEEN WHOM?

Moreover also I gave them my sabbaths, to be *a sign between me and them,* that they might know that I am the LORD that sanctify them....

I am the LORD your God; walk in my statutes, and keep my judgments, and do them;

And hallow my sabbaths; and they shall be *a sign between me and you,* that ye may know that I am the LORD your God.

Ezekiel 20:12, 19, 20

WHAT IF MAN'S TEACHING IS CONTRARY TO GOD'S LAW?

Then Peter and the other apostles answered and said, *We ought to obey God rather than men.* Acts 5:29

WHOM DID JESUS SAY WE SHOULD SERVE?

Then saith Jesus unto him, Get thee hence, Satan: for it is written, *Thou shalt worship the Lord thy God, and him only shalt thou serve.*
Matthew 4:10

WHAT ARE THE ONLY TWO CHOICES THAT WE HAVE?

Know ye not, that to whom ye yield yourselves servants to obey, his servants ye are to whom ye *obey*; whether of *sin unto death*, or of *obedience unto righteousness*? *Romans 6:16*

WHAT ARE WE TOLD TO DO?

Now therefore fear the LORD, and serve him in sincerity and in truth: and put away the gods which your fathers served on the other side of the flood, and in Egypt; and *serve ye the LORD.*

And if it seem evil unto you to serve the LORD, *choose you this day whom ye will serve*; whether the gods which your fathers served that were on the other side of the flood, or the gods of the Amorites, in whose land ye dwell: but *as for me and my house, we will serve the LORD.* Joshua 24:14, 15

WHAT SHOULD OUR RESPONSE BE?

And the people said unto Joshua, *The LORD our God will we serve, and his voice will we obey. Joshua 24:24*

THE FIRST DAY IN THE NEW TESTAMENT

There are only eight texts in the entire New Testament that refer to the first day of the week. This study will consider each of them.

WHY DOES MATTHEW SAY THEY CAME ON THE FIRST DAY?

In the end of the sabbath, as it began to dawn toward *the first day* of the week, came Mary Magdalene and the other Mary to see the sepulchre. *Matthew 28:1*

WHY DOES MARK SAY THE WOMEN CAME TO THE TOMB?

And when the sabbath was past, Mary Magdalene, and Mary the mother of James, and Salome, had *bought sweet spices, that they might come and anoint him.*

And very early in the morning the *first day* of the week, they came unto the sepulchre at the rising of the sun. *Mark 16:1, 2*

WHAT DOES THIS THIRD REFERENCE SAY HAPPENED?

Now when *Jesus was risen* early *the first day* of the week, he appeared first to Mary Magdalene, out of whom he had cast seven devils. *Mark 16:9*

WERE THE DISCIPLES CELEBRATING THE RESURRECTION?

And she went and told them that had been with him, as *they mourned and wept.*

And they, when they had heard that he was alive, and had been seen of her, *believed not.*

After that he appeared in another form unto two of them, as they walked, and went into the country.

And they went and told it unto the residue: *neither believed they them.*

Afterward he appeared unto the eleven as they sat at meat, and *upbraided [rebuked] them with their unbelief and hardness of heart, because they believed not them which had seen him after he was risen.*   *Mark 16:10-14*

DOES LUKE INDICATE A CHANGE OF THE SABBATH?

Now upon *the first* day of the week, very early in the morning, they came unto the sepulchre, bringing the spices which they had prepared, and certain others with them. *Luke 24:1*

DOES JOHN SAY THE FIRST DAY REPLACED THE SABBATH?

The *first day* of the week cometh Mary Magdalene early, when it was yet dark, unto the sepulchre, and seeth the stone taken away from the sepulchre. *John 20:1*

> NOTE: Every one of these references clearly reveal that the women came to the tomb on Sunday morning to do a work they would not do on the holy Sabbath and transgress the commandment of God.

WHY WERE THE DISCIPLES ASSEMBLED TOGETHER?

Then *the same day at evening, being the first day* of the week, when the doors were shut where *the disciples were assembled for fear of the Jews,* came Jesus and stood in the midst, and saith unto them, Peace be unto you. *John 20:19*

WHY WERE THERE "MANY LIGHTS" AS PAUL PREACHED?

And upon *the first day* of the week, when the disciples came together to break bread, *Paul* preached unto them, ready to depart on the morrow; and *continued his speech until midnight.*

And *there were many lights* in the upper chamber, where they were gathered together.

And there sat in a window a certain young man named Eutychus, being fallen into a deep sleep: and as Paul was long preaching, he sunk down with sleep, and fell down from the third loft, and was taken up dead.

And Paul went down, and fell on him, and embracing him said, Trouble not yourselves; for his life is in him. *Acts 20:7-10*

NOTE: This is a Saturday night meeting that continued until dawn on Sunday morning. (See the New English Bible or any commentary.) In the Bible a day begins with the evening (Genesis 1:5, 8, 13, etc.; Leviticus 23:32). We still follow this practice for certain holidays such as Christmas and New Year's Eve.

WHAT DID PAUL DO AT SUNRISE SUNDAY MORNING?

When he therefore was come up again, and had broken bread, and eaten, and talked a long while, even till break of day, so *he departed....*

And we went before to ship, and sailed unto Assos, there intending to take in Paul: for so had he appointed, minding himself to go *afoot.*

And when he *met with us at Assos*, we took him in, and came to Mitylene. *Acts 20:11, 13, 14*

NOTE: On Sunday Paul walked 20 miles to meet the other disciples at Assos. This is something he would never have done on the Sabbath.

DOES THE LAST TEXT REFER TO CHANGING THE SABBATH?

Now *concerning the collection for the saints*, as I have given order to the churches of Galatia, even so do ye.

Upon the *first day* of the week let every one of you *lay by him in store*, as God hath prospered him, *that there be no gatherings when I come. 1 Corinthians 16:1, 2*

NOTE: Paul informed all of the churches, including Corinth, of the need of laying aside money at home for the poor believers in Jerusalem so that when he passed through he could readily pick it up to take to them. (See

Acts 11:29, 30; Romans 15:25, 26).

WHAT DOES THE FOURTH COMMANDMENT SAY TO DO?
Remember the sabbath day, to keep it holy. **Exodus 20:8**

CAN WE REPLACE THE COMMANDMENTS FOR TRADITION?
But he answered and said unto them, *Why do ye also transgress the commandment of God by your tradition?...*
Thus have *ye made the commandment of God of none effect by your tradition....*
But *in vain they do worship me, teaching for doctrines the commandments of men.* **Matthew 15:3, 6, 9**

IF WE LOVE JESUS WHAT SHOULD WE DO?
If ye love me, keep my commandments. **John 14:15**

HOW TO KEEP THE SABBATH

WHAT ACTIVITIES DID JESUS DO ON THE SABBATH?
And when *the Sabbath day* was come, he began to *teach in the synagogue*: and many hearing him were astonished, saying, From whence hath this man these things? and what wisdom is this which is given unto him, that even such mighty works are wrought by his hands? *Mark 6:2*

WAS IT COMMON FOR HIM TO ATTEND SABBATH SERVICES?
And he came to Nazareth, where he had been brought up: and, *as his custom was, he went into the synagogue on the Sabbath day,* and stood up for to read. *Luke 4:16*

WHAT ELSE SHOULD ONE DO ON THE SABBATH?
And, behold, there was a man which had his hand withered. And they asked him, saying, Is it *lawful to heal on the sabbath*

days? that they might accuse him.

And he said unto them, What man shall there be among you, that shall have one sheep, and if it fall into a pit on the Sabbath day, will he not lay hold on it, and lift it out?

How much then is a man better than a sheep? Wherefore *it is lawful to do well on the sabbath days.*

Then saith he to the man, Stretch forth thine hand. And he stretched it forth; and it was restored whole, like as the other.

Then the Pharisees went out, and held a council against him, how they might destroy him. But when Jesus knew it, he withdrew himself from thence: and *great multitudes followed him, and he healed them all; Matthew 12:10-15*

WHAT BRINGS GOD'S PROMISED BLESSING?

Blessed is the man that doeth this, and the son of man that layeth hold on it; that *keepeth the Sabbath from polluting it,* and keepeth his hand from doing any evil. *Isaiah 56:2*

WHAT MUST WE "REMEMBER" TO DO WITH THE SABBATH?

Remember the Sabbath day, to keep it holy. Exodus 20:8

WHAT ARE WE TO REFRAIN FROM ON THE HOLY SABBATH?

Six days shalt thou labour, and do all thy work:

But the seventh day is the Sabbath of the LORD thy God: *in it thou shalt not do any work*, thou, nor thy son, nor thy daughter, thy manservant, nor thy maidservant, nor thy cattle, nor thy stranger that is within thy gates:

For in six days the LORD made heaven and earth, the sea, and all that in them is, and rested the seventh day: wherefore *the LORD blessed the Sabbath day, and hallowed it. Exodus 20:9-11*

WHY WERE THE JEWS CARRIED INTO CAPTIVITY?

In those days saw I in Judah some treading wine presses *on the Sabbath*, and bringing in sheaves, and lading asses; as also wine, grapes, and figs, and all manner of burdens, which they brought into Jerusalem *on the Sabbath* day: and *I testified against them* in the day wherein they sold victuals [food].

There dwelt men of Tyre also therein, which brought fish, and all manner of ware, and *sold on the Sabbath* unto the children of Judah, and in Jerusalem.

Then *I contended with the nobles of Judah*, and said unto them, What *evil thing* is this that ye do, and *profane the Sabbath day*?

Did not your fathers thus, and did not our God bring all this evil upon us, and upon this city? yet *ye bring more wrath upon Israel by profaning the Sabbath. Nehemiah 13:15-18*

WHAT CAN WE LEARN FROM ISRAEL'S UNBELIEF?

For he spake in a certain place of the seventh day on this wise, And *God did rest the seventh day from all his works....
There remaineth therefore a rest to the people of God.*

For he that is entered into his rest, he also hath *ceased from his own works, as God did from his.* Let us labour therefore to *enter into that rest, lest any man fall after the same example of unbelief.   Hebrews 4:4, 9-11*

WHAT DOES GOD WANT ALL PEOPLE TO DO?

Also the sons of the stranger, that *join themselves* to the LORD, *to serve him,* and to *love* the name of the LORD, to *be his servants*, every one that *keepeth the Sabbath from polluting it*, and taketh hold of my covenant; *Isaiah 56:6*

WHAT DOES GOD WANT US TO DO WITH HIS LAW?

And they that shall be of thee shall build the old waste places: thou shalt *raise up the foundations of many generations*; and thou shalt be called, The *repairer of the breach*, The *restorer of paths to dwell in. Isaiah 58:12*

WHAT IS THE WAY TO RESTORE THE BREAK IN GOD'S LAW?

If thou *turn away thy foot from [stop trampling on] the Sabbath*, from *doing thy pleasure on my holy day*; and call the Sabbath a delight, the holy of the LORD, honourable; and shalt honour him, *not doing thine own ways, nor finding thine own pleasure, nor speaking thine own words*: *Isaiah 58:13*

> NOTE: The Sabbath is holy time and we are to "remember" this day "to keep it holy" (Exodus 20:8-11). Following is a review of some of the Bible examples.
>
> 1. Attend religious services. Jesus' custom was to attend religious services (Luke 4:16). Paul's custom was the same as his Lord's (Acts 17:1, 2). Early Christians attended services every Sabbath (Act 18:4).
> 2. Refrain from secular labor and academic pursuits. Do not cause others to work (Exodus 20:8-11).
> 3. Study God's word (Matthew 12:10-15).
> 4. Do good. Reach out to others. Heal the sick. Visit shut-ins (Isaiah 56:2).
> 5. Do not buy or sell (Nehemiah 13:15-18; Ezekiel 22:26).
> 6. This would include food as well as other items (Nehemiah 13:15, 16).
> 7. Minister to the less fortunate (Isaiah 58:7, 8).
> 8. Not seek our own pleasure (Isaiah 58:13).
> 9. Even our words should be guarded (Isaiah 58:12-14).
> 10. Spend some time in nature, God's second lesson book (Psalms 111:2, 3; Job 12:7-9).
> 11. Spend quality time with the family.
> 12. Contemplate the cross of Christ and His great love for you.

BOOKS BY JOE W. GRESHAM

DEALING WITH THE DEVIL'S DECEPTION-HOW TO CHOOSE A BIBLE

An overview of the development and dangers of the modern translations of the Bible and the men and motives behind them.

Over four and a half centuries ago the great reformer, Martin Luther, said, "No greater mischief can happen to a Christian people than to have God's word taken from them, or have it so falsified that they no longer have it pure and clear. God grant that we and our descendants be not witnesses of such a calamity."

Is it possible that we, today, are witnessing just such a calamity? The answer and issues will become extremely clear when you finish Dealing With the Devil's Deception.

THE DEVIL'S DECEPTION ABOUT DEATH

Where are our beloved dead? Where do people really go at death? Do they haunt houses? Are they reincarnated? Do they perhaps go to some place called limbo or purgatory? Could it be that they are simply floating around on a little pink cloud strumming a harp? Are they possibly in heaven or hell? All of these are prominent teachings in the world today. Every religious group (and even the non-religious) believe one or more of the above.

Why is it that so many people believe such a conflicting array of thoughts concerning the same topic? Could it be that so few go to the Bible to find truth and are simply content to unquestionably accept what someone else has told them without individual investigation?

The Bible gives very clear and distinct answers to this mystery. Therefore, this book will trace what the Bible teaches and expose *The Devil's Deception About Death.*

A FAITH THAT WORKS
A simple, yet systematic, verse-by-verse study of the book of James.

In the midst of all the confusion and dissension over the relationship between faith and works this book clearly and with simplicity presents the biblical correlation concerning the two imperatives of the Christian faith.

FOOD FIGHTS
The Bible declares: "Beloved, I wish above all things that thou mayest prosper and be in health" (3 John 1:2). Yet it is a sorrowful reality that so many today have tremendous, often fatal, health problems; most of which could be prevented, reversed, and even cured by following simple Bible guidelines.

Whereas food fights can be fun for children, for adults they can be fatal. This little book examines what the Bible says on the subject of food and how many today respond to what God says about food that kills. It presents a thoughtful analysis of the so-called "problem texts" pertaining to this subject that will clarify the confusion and dissolve the delusions.

THE FORGOTTEN COMMANDMENT
It is interesting that the only commandment God prefaced with "remember" is the one the majority of the world has forgotten. When God brings this commandment to one's attention they are usually told by their religious leaders not to concern themselves with it for it is now obsolete. This, however, should not come as a surprise for the word of God warned that there would be "false teachers" who would "bring in damnable heresies" and "many shall follow their pernicious ways" and the "truth shall be evil spoken of" (2 Peter 2:1-2). This has truly taken place today. Discover how in *The Forgotten Commandment.*

GOD'S LAST MESSAGE TO EARTH

A simple, yet systematic, verse-by-verse study of the book of Revelation.

Many claim the book of Revelation cannot be understood and that it was never intended to be. The very title of the book, however, refutes this claim, for it is a revelation or revealing.

There is so much in this book God would have His people come to understand that they might prepare themselves and shape their course of action, so as to escape the plagues that are to shortly fall upon the world. His promise is "Blessed is he that readeth, and they that hear the words of this prophecy, and keep those things which are written therein" (Revelation 1:3).

THE GOOD NEWS OF GALATIANS

A simple, yet systematic, verse-by-verse study of the book of Galatians.

The glorious good news of the gospel, in Galatians, reveals the power of God that enables the believer to live a victorious life in Christ.

MODERN PROPHETS

A comparison of the real versus the counterfeit of a much neglected Bible teaching that has been ignored, rejected, and corrupted within Christianity - the gift of prophecy.

Jesus gave repeated warning about false prophets, thus emphasizing a counterfeit of a genuine gift. (Matthew 7:15, 16; 24:11, 24) This subject is so vital that the apostle Paul admonished: "Quench not the Spirit. Despise not prophesyings. Prove all things; hold fast that which is good" (1 Thessalonians 5:19-21). "Beloved, believe not every spirit" is the apostle John's admonition, "but try the spirits whether they are of God: because many false prophets are gone out into the world" (1 John 4:1).

Is the gift of prophecy to be found in the church today? How are we to try or test one thought to possess this gift? How can one tell the true from the false? The Bible speaks decisively on this subject and gives several tests by which one can tell a true prophet from a false one.

SIMPLIFIED STUDIES OF THE SACRED SCRIPTURES
Question and answer studies of many of the great doctrines and prophecies of God's word presented in a simplified and easy-to-understand format.

This 296 page book is an excellent tool for personal study or Bible study classes. It is filled with Scripture to provide you with answers to nearly all your questions on Bible topics.

WHICH GOSPEL?
A treatise of "the everlasting gospel" and how it has been and is being perverted within Christianity.

The word of God makes it clear that the gospel "is the power of God unto salvation." But do we truly understand what the gospel is or the power it has for us today? With the prevailing perversions of the gospel today, can the people of God really discover which gospel contains this life-changing power and how to experience it? This book presents the truths of the gospel in such a way as is seldom seen in the Christian world today, revealing God's purpose in the plan of salvation from the atonement to the reception of the redeemed. From justification to the future of God's Remnant church, this book reveals the power of the Holy Spirit and the assurance that what God has promised, He is able also to perform.

WHY SO MANY DENOMINATIONS
Have you ever wondered, if there's one God and one Bible, why there are so many different churches that dot the hillsides? The world has thousands upon thousands of church congregations and with this multitude of denominations people often wonder: "How can I find the truth? How can I know what truth is?" With this collection of confusing concepts how can one

discover truth? The Bible clearly describes why there are so many different denominations and it helps us find our way through the maze of confusion. It helps intelligent, thinking, rational people to understand where these churches came from, and how to sort out truth from error. As one studies Bible prophecy they will understand what happened to the early Christian church, why it happened, and discover how to find truth for themselves.

THE WISE SHALL UNDERSTAND
A verse-by-verse study of the book of Daniel presented in a simple, easy-to-understand manner.

Of all the books of the Bible, Daniel speaks most repeatedly of last day events and claims to pertain directly to the "time of the end" (Daniel 12:4, 6, 8, 9, 13). The things written in Daniel were written specifically for those of us living today. Now, as never before, it is necessary for us to understand this book. As for those who say it cannot be understood, I would caution them to beware, lest they find themselves calling God a liar, for He has declared in no uncertain terms that "none of the wicked shall understand; but the wise shall understand" (Daniel 12:10).

BOOKLETS FOR SHARING

THE ANTICHRIST AND THE MARK OF THE BEAST

One of the most awesome warnings ever given in the Bible says: "If any man worship the beast and his image, and receive his mark in his forehead, or in his hand, the same shall drink of the wine of the wrath of God, which is poured out without mixture into the cup of his indignation; and he shall be tormented with fire and brimstone in the presence of the holy angels, and in the presence of the Lamb: And the smoke of their torment ascendeth up for ever and ever: and they have no rest day nor night, who worship the beast and his image, and whosoever receiveth the mark of his name." (Revelation 14:9-11)

The identity of this power is so intricately detailed in the prophetic books of Daniel and Revelation that none need be confused or uncertain as to who it is, when it is to arise, how long it is to rule, what it will do, and what will eventually become of it. Understanding these things is essential to knowing what the "mark of the beast" is and how to avoid receiving it.

There are 17 different distinguishing points clearly identifying this apostate power presented in this book.

ARMAGEDDON AND THE PLAGUES

In Revelation chapter fifteen we are introduced to the seven last plagues that culminate in the Battle of Armageddon. These plagues contain God's final judgement which is poured upon the world just before the return of Jesus to take his people home. But before Jesus comes God reveals to John the results of these awesome judgements and shows him those that will survive the plagues. What are these fearsome plagues? How close are we to the Battle of Armageddon? And how can we survive the future? These are questions that are answered in this little book. You will be able to face the future with assurance.

THE ATONEMENT AND THE CLEANSING OF THE SANCTUARY

The urgency of the following inspired statement has prompted the printing of this little book.

"The subject of the sanctuary and the investigative judgment should be clearly understood by the people of God. All need a knowledge for themselves of the position and work of their great High Priest. Otherwise it will be impossible for them to exercise the faith which is essential at this time or to occupy the position which God designs them to fill." *The Great Controversy,* p. 488

BIBLE STUDIES MADE EASY

Outline studies of many of the great doctrines of the Bible presented in a clear and concise manner.

An excellent tool for personal study or for sharing your faith.

CHRISTIAN PERFECTION - DOES GOD EXPECT TOO MUCH?

Jesus came to this world bearing in His flesh the results of sin, but in His humanity was able to live a life free of sin. In His human nature He was able to overcome all temptations to sin that Satan hurled at Him, and He says to each of us: "To him that overcometh will I grant to sit with me in my throne, even as I also overcame, and am set down with my Father in his throne." (Revelation 3:21) Is this possible? Can we overcome all sin, every temptation, even as Jesus did? God says, YES; Satan says, NO. Whom shall we believe?

THE CITY OF GOD

John said he "saw the holy city, new Jerusalem, coming down from God out of heaven" (Revelation 21:2). The real beauty of this glorious city is not found in the golden streets, gates of pearl, or walls of many precious jewels; but something of far more inestimable excellence than all these combined.

73

DEFYING THE DEATH DECREE

A study of the great golden image of Daniel three and the parallel to the image to be established in Revelation 13:14 when again the death decree will go forth that "as many as would not worship the image of the beast should be killed" (Revelation 13:15).

THE DESIRE OF AGES STUDY GUIDE
A study and chain reference of The Desire of Ages
A study of the human nature of Jesus and the power of the Holy Spirit to live the victorious, sinless life of Christ.

THE DIABOLIC DANGERS AND DOCTRINAL DESTRUCTION IN THE MODERN BIBLE VERSIONS

Upon investigation of the modern translations, it immediately becomes evident they often contain variant readings. For example, if a person were to take five different translations of the Bible and turn to Hosea 13:9, they would probably find all five translations say something totally different, as can be seen from the following examples.

O Israel, thou hast destroyed thyself; but in me is thine help. (KJV). I will destroy you, O Israel; who can help you? (RSV). I will destroy you, O Israel, because you are against me, against your helper. (NIV). O Israel, if I destroy you, who can save you? (LB). It is your destruction, O Israel, That you are against Me, against your help. (NASB).

The question that naturally arises is: "Which one is correct?" If a person has four Bibles and they all read differently, can they all be the "word of God?" How can one tell truth from error? This book presents many of the doctrinal dangers in the modern translations.

THE GLORIOUS FUTURE OF THE REMNANT CHURCH

When the renowned Christian writer E.G. White said that those "who do not feel grieved over their own spiritual

74

declension, nor mourn over the sins of others, will be left without the seal of God," the reference was to a biblical principle and teaching that many today reject and ridicule. But as with all other teachings of God's word, the opposition of the obstinate or rejection of the rebellious do not nullify its veracity. References to this Bible teaching are too numerous to ignore or misunderstand and the response of the Remnant Church to the claims that "the people of God are numbered with Babylon," and "the loud cry is a call to come out of her" are of such relevance that it demands our candid consideration.

GOD'S SORROW, OUR SHAME - LET THE PROPHET SPEAK

Various theories have been set forth as to what actually took place at the 1888 General Conference Session in Minneapolis, but many questions still demand straight answers. 1) Did God send a special message to His people 100 years ago? 2) Was the message accepted or rejected? 3) What was this message? Can we know for certain today or did God allow it to be lost for all eternity? 4) Were Jones and Waggoner "trouble makers" as some claim or were they "Christ's delegated messengers"? 5) What was Ellen White's position in the midst of all this turmoil? Just where did the prophet stand? 6) Do the events in the lives of Jones and Waggoner in later years have any bearing on the message they brought to the church in 1888?

This little book presents a documented, historical overview of what took place in Minneapolis and the response to the message in the ensuing years.

THE JUDGMENT AND THE CLEANSING OF THE SANCTUARY

When, where, and how does the judgment take place? Where is Jesus now? What is He doing? Why hasn't He come back yet? What does the Bible mean when it says "Unto two thousand and three hundred days; then shall the sanctuary be cleansed?" (Daniel 8:14) These and many other questions are answered in this little book.

THE KINGS OF THE NORTH AND SOUTH

The prophecy of the Kings of the north and south contain a history that is most essential to understand in order to fully comprehend God's workings among the nations of the world. As we behold how these things have been fulfilled just as God said they would be, we can have full confidence and assurance about those things which lie ahead. Furthermore, if we do not know the historical background of the kings of the north and south it would be impossible to know if they exist today, their identities, how they will meet their end, or when this event is to take place.

This book follows a very important biblical principle of prophetic interpretation: everything should be considered as literal, unless it is obviously symbolic. Because of a failure to adhere to this principle, there have been a variety of views pertaining to this prophecy. Some claim, for example, the king of the north is Turkey, others that it is the Papacy, some that it is Russia, and still others that it is Satan himself. This confusion need not exist (and indeed would not exist), if people would cease to place their own fanciful interpretation on various passages.

Thus, this book allows the Scripture to be its own interpreter and apply the information contained in God's word to a literal, chronological, historical setting.

THE MEN, MOTIVES AND MALICIOUS MUTILATIONS BEHIND THE MODERN BIBLE VERSIONS

With the multiplicity of modern Bibles today we discover there are between 5,000 and 36,000 changes in the modern Bibles, depending upon the version one chooses. In addition to this there are over 200 cases in which a verse's authenticity is questioned by complete omission, or a footnote, in the modern translations. These various changes affect approximately five percent of the Scriptures, which to some may not appear to be such a large percentage; but it amounts to more than the omission of the entire gospel of John, which is only three percent. It further causes people to doubt and to question what does and does not actually belong in the Bible. For example the NASB contains 4,000 significant additions, subtractions and changes; whereas the NIV contains 6,653 and has 64,094 less words than the KJV.

This book will consider those involved with the manipulation and mutilation of the Bible and reveal their secular approach and handling of the Sacred Scriptures, some of the changes they made, why they made those changes, and how they have destroyed Bible doctrine. You will be both appalled and outraged when you see these crazed critics shredding the word of God, and then officiously piecing it back together with thousands upon thousands of additions, deletions and perversions.

THE MILLENNIUM

The millennium is a subject that has for years arrested the attention of people world wide. The word itself does not appear in the Bible, but comes from a compound of two Latin words "mille" and "annum," which means simply, "thousand years." This thousand-year period, called the millennium, is mentioned six times in the first seven verses of Revelation chapter twenty and refers to that period of time in which Satan is to be bound and perfect peace and happiness will reign in the universe.

There are many various theories regarding the millennium which have been based largely upon speculations and fictitious novels. Some have even claimed that the devil has already been bound and we are now in the millennium. To this insanity a minister once replied, "If the devil is bound, he must be tied with a rubber chain that stretches from Paris to Bombay and from Washington, D.C. to the Kremlin." All we need to do is look about us to see that the devil has never been more active than he is today. This is why the Word of God warns us, "Be sober, be vigilant; because your adversary the devil, as a roaring lion, walketh about, seeking whom he may devour" (1 Peter 5:8).

This book will reveal there is no reason for anyone to experience confusion or uncertainty in regard to the millennium, for the Bible speaks quite clearly and in much detail on this subject presenting most clear, concise, and concrete statements pertaining to this thousand-year period.

THE NATURE OF CHRIST AND THE SPIRIT OF ANTICHRIST

Over a century ago a very gifted Christian writer, E.G. White, declared: "In our conclusions, we make many mistakes because of our erroneous views of the human nature of our Lord. When we give to His human nature a power that is not possible for man to have in his conflicts with Satan, we destroy the completeness of His humanity."

This little book presents an overview of this most vital subject and enables the people of God to see their way through the "erroneous views" and avoid the "many mistakes" that are so prevalent today.

OLD HERESIES AND NEW THEOLOGY - THE MISCONCEPTION OF SIN

What is it about sin that makes it so bad? The Bible is clear that sin is something so deadly that it claimed the very life of the Son of God. (Isaiah 53:1-12; Hebrews 9:28) However, there is much confusion on this subject today. Many have a very limited and often perverted concept of what sin is and its tremendous impact on both God and man. This book is designed to solidify the believer in the biblical teaching about sin that they not be deceived by the many false, man-made theories that are circulating within the Christian community today.

PANORAMA OF PROPHECY

The book of Daniel is a most unique book in that it contains several step-by-step prophecies of world empires from the seventh century B.C. to the very day in which we are now living. These prophecies are some of the most easily understood found in the Scriptures and cover nearly 2600 years of history in absolute accuracy. As one commentator has stated: "Human wisdom has never devised so brief a record that embraced so much. Human language never set forth in so few words such a great volume of historical truth. The finger of God is here. Let us heed the lesson well."

THE SECRET OF THE RAPTURE: WILL YOU BE LEFT BEHIND?

Since publication of the *Left Behind* series of books, the release of *Left Behind: The Movie*, and the October 2014 release of the movie *Left Behind*, there has been an explosion of interest in the sensational and speculative errors being promoted by the movies and the books upon which they are based. This has resulted in many being deceived into thinking these false (and admittedly fictional) concepts are actually Bible truth. *The Secret of the Rapture* is designed to offset these false and fanciful theories and enable people to see the beauty and truth of the coming of Christ. This little book will strengthen your understanding and faith concerning the "blessed hope, and the glorious appearing of the great God and our Saviour Jesus Christ" (Titus 2:13), as well as enable you to share this great Bible truth with those who are being deceived by the errors being propagated today.

SIGNS OF THE SAVIOR'S SOON COMING

Jesus' disciples gathered with Him on the Mount of Olives and inquired: "Tell us, when shall these things be? and what shall be the sign of thy coming, and of the end of the world?" (Matthew 24:3). The word of God responds to this question with no less than 53 prophetic events.

In speaking of His coming, Jesus said, "when ye shall see all these things, know that it is near, even at the doors." Matthew 24:33 This little book was prepared that all may "see" and "know" that the "blessed hope, and the glorious appearing of the great God and our Saviour Jesus Christ" (Titus 2:13) is closer than many believe.

A STARTLING DREAM

This little book explores one of the most easily understood prophecies found in the Scriptures. It covers nearly 2600 years of history in absolute accuracy, and as one commentator has stated: "Human wisdom has never devised so brief a record that embraced so much. Human language never set forth in so few words such a great volume of historical truth. The finger of God is here. Let us heed the lesson well." Smith, *The Prophecies of Daniel and the Revelation, p. 39.*

THE TWO SIDES OF JUSTIFICATION

Few today have truly understood the depth of what was accomplished at the cross or what motivated such a selfless sacrifice. Although many believe there is unanimity among Christians pertaining to the justification that came through the shedding of the precious blood of God's Son, in reality there is much diversity concerning who has been justified, as well as how and when justification takes place. This little book explores the initiative of God in the redemption of fallen humanity.

WHY SUFFERING AND DEATH

As we look about us today, we see a world that is filled with sickness, suffering, sorrow, pain and death. Encompassed with agony people cry out "Why does God allow these things to happen? Why does He cause so much affliction and anguish?" He is often blamed for things for which He is not responsible and which were never a part of His plan for planet earth and its inhabitants.

JOE W. GRESHAM IS AVAILABLE FOR:
Camp meetings   Workshops/Retreats
Churches/Seminars

To schedule please contact:
Fourth Angel Ministries
P.O. Box 136637
Fort Worth, Texas 76136
817-919-7267
Fourthangelbooks@aol.com
www.fourthangelministries.com